MAPPING THE IMAGINARY

ALA Editions purchases fund advocacy,
awareness, and accreditation programs
for library professionals worldwide.

MAPPING THE IMAGINARY

Supporting Creative Writers through Programming, Prompts, and Research

Riley Hanick, Micah Bateman, and Jennifer Burek Pierce

FOREWORD BY

Elizabeth McCracken

ALA
Editions

Chicago | 2019

© 2019 by the American Library Association

Extensive effort has gone into ensuring the reliability of the information in this book; however, the publisher makes no warranty, express or implied, with respect to the material contained herein.

ISBN: 978-0-8389-1841-8 (paper)

Library of Congress Cataloging-in-Publication Data on file.

Cover design by Alejandra Diaz.

♾ This paper meets the requirements of ANSI/NISO Z39.48–1992 (Permanence of Paper).

Printed in the United States of America

23 22 21 20 19   5 4 3 2 1

For every writer still to come—RH

For my mother, the teacher—MB

*For Kate, storyteller, and in memory of
Bev, editor—JBP*

CONTENTS

7
PLACE AND SPACE

8
POETRY AND VERSE

CONCLUSION

APPENDIXES

FOREWORD

I n some ways I made the most consequential decision of my life when I was fifteen years old, and walked into the Newton Free Library in Newton Corner, Massachusetts, to ask for a job shelving books. The rest of my life and all its forks in the road seem to lead from the day I decided to join my fortunes to the library's. I was put to work among books and book people, and there I have remained, in one way or other, ever since. In the rambling, odd-shaped old building, I was assigned to shelve fiction A–SM. The only bad thing I can say about my shelving beat is that the library interfiled authors whose surnames began with Mac or Mc, so that MacDonald and McDonald were next to each other, and I found this boneheaded. Insulting, even.

The Newton Free Library had a poetry series, which was how as a teenager I saw Maxine Kumin read in the All-Purpose Room (not a room at all, just a space upstairs constructed out of shelves, just off the 800s). I think this must have been the first poetry reading I ever attended, and the anthology from the library's spring poetry festival the first anthology I ever bought that was not assigned to me. Somebody at the library took poetry seriously: in 1982, while filling in for a fellow library page who'd called in sick, I shelved the new nonfiction, including an intriguing collection of poetry called *The Incognito Lounge*, which was the first time I ever read the work of Denis Johnson.

I think every aspiring writer should shelve books in a public library: there is no other way to develop the proper balance of awe and nonchalance at the physical object that is a book. Shelf-reading is excellent, too, for finding books you had no idea you were looking for. But serendipity is no substitute for a relationship with the librarians: reference, reader's advisory, and circulation librarians, who combine serendipity with a professional magnetism: they do not merely search for books, they attract them.

The library attracted writers, too, who came to research in the reference room, a place that in my memory is as soaring and windowed as a cathedral, though the only thing I can be sure of is that it led to the periodical room and the stacks. Certainly the first event I ever did as a published author was a fund-raiser for the Newton Free Library. I almost never put actual people into my work, but a version of that terrible old building appears in my first novel: its glass-floored stacks, its oddball patrons and employees, its possibilities and civic seriousness, its architectural lumbago.

The second public library of my life was the main library in Somerville, Massachusetts, where I was the circulation desk chief after getting my MLIS. The Somerville Public Library's All Purpose Room was an actual room, with a door, and there I had the good luck to teach a couple of creative writing classes, on both fiction and memoir, to, as it was always put, The Community. The community just meant writers. The classes were free. The only thing the students had in common was the library itself: they'd come in the front door and seen the sign. Public libraries are chock-full of people and books and recordings and art that have nothing in common except the library itself, which has collected and organized them. Those classes were among the most rewarding teaching experiences of my life, because nobody showed up who wasn't serious, and also game, the two requirements for any good writer. One class member was a serious writer who was homeless and went on to publish a book about his life on the streets; another was a woman whose daughter had just turned four, and who was returning to her dream of writing fiction.

This book is an excellent guide for what to do with the writers and readers who come through the door of your library—including those patrons who don't know they're writers yet. There is no greater necessity to writers than material, and no place warehouses more material than the library. This book will help bring material—and ideas, and methods, and new books—to creative writers of all sorts, so that they might in return dream of their own work in their own beloved library.

—*Elizabeth McCracken*
November 13, 2018

ACKNOWLEDGMENTS

The authors warmly acknowledge the origins of this book in a NerdCon: Stories presentation with Colleen Theisen, who is now chief curator of exhibitions, programs, and education at Syracuse University Libraries, and Becky Canovan, assistant director of public services at the University of Dubuque. Our panel, "Write Your Own Hamilton: Finding Your Story in Libraries," launched this book. We appreciate, too, the trust of the organizers of NerdCon: Stories (Minneapolis, 2016) in selecting us to present there; many thanks to Valerie Barr of VidCon and Complexly, LLC, in particular. The librarians and writers in the audience offered a dynamic response, and their questions, together with the keen interest of our ALA Editions editor, Jamie Santoro, furthered the sense that there was more to say on this subject.

Librarians and librarians have supported this project since NerdCon, too. We want to thank Beth Kamp of the Ramstein Library at Ramstein Air Force Base (Germany) for her questions about how writers' groups could advise participants on revision, which prompted us to develop our guidelines on group critiques. We want to acknowledge the interest of Madeline Jarvis, adult and information services coordinator at the Marion Public Library (Iowa), in related programming.

Thanks also go to the University of Iowa's International Writing Program, and particularly to Christopher Merrill and

Susannah Shive, for informing our thinking about massive open online courses and popular/public creative writing pedagogy. We owe further gratitude to Profs. Dee Morris and Ed Folsom at the University of Iowa, whose teaching was integral to our chapters touching on documentary poetry and Walt Whitman, respectively. We are likewise grateful to Elizabeth McCracken, gifted writer and generous instructor, for her stories and guiding words.

Many thanks to those with whom we shared both ideas and creative writing classrooms across multiple states and years. We also appreciate the individuals whose technical and editorial support enabled our production of this manuscript, including Danielle Wheeler and the staff at ALA Editions.

The University of Iowa provided a 2018 Graduate College Summer Fellowship to Riley Hanick, which was another plank supporting the development of this project. Thanks as well to the University of Texas at Austin for providing support to Micah Bateman as part of the Andrew W. Mellon Engaged Scholar Initiative.

INTRODUCTION

Libraries and Writers

Everyone has a story to tell. Whether we consider archives of contemporary audio recordings, like StoryCorps; ever-increasing lists of new memoirs; or the exchanges that unfold through online media, sharing words and ideas with others is a facet of our lives. Librarians have been and remain associated with the world of stories—printed, bound, and shelved—among the holdings they help patrons navigate. Now, information professionals and educators can also help patrons find their own stories in libraries—not only as readers, but as writers, too.

Given the centrality of acquiring and preserving stories to our profession, it is worth considering the past in relation to this moment. Where authorship was once an uncommon enterprise, undertaken by individuals who were either daring or desperate, in the twentieth century it became a more attractive occupation. The legends and publicity that accrued to authors like Ernest Hemingway and James Baldwin, living as expatriates in Paris, evoked a sense of glamor and possibility. With the inception of creative writing programs in universities and their widespread growth during the second half of the century, it was increasingly normal to view the creation of fiction, poetry, and eventually creative nonfiction as professions like any other, the result of education and specialized training. While literary publishing has been permanently transformed by the program era, popular perceptions of the writing life have also continued to evolve, since contemporary writers of all genres and ages can now easily create narratives of real or imagined lives, sharing them via myriad electronic and print outlets. How the activities that have defined our field might change in response to the new dynamics of authorship underlies this book.

Numbers are one means of documenting the profound contemporary interest in authorship, signaling a shift that libraries should consider as they evaluate their goals and strategies for community engagement. National Novel Writing Month, or NaNoWriMo, which began in 1999 and now sees well over 400,000 participants each November, is one manifestation of this broad contemporary interest.[1] From San Francisco to Chicago, there are poetry centers committed to supporting new voices and living writers. National Public Radio has drawn attention to Narratio, an online site that supports "young people from around the world," particularly those displaced by war and famine, by encouraging them to "submit poems, essays, and stories" and hosting workshops that facilitate their path to publication.[2] More generally, the number of blogs is beyond reckoning, with Tumblr alone hosting an estimated 345 million individual outlets.[3] These impressive signs of the writing impulse, together with indications that people are also reading more books, particularly poetry, offer a rationale for working with people who want to create as well as consume the written word.[4]

Information literacy experts advise that we prepare patrons to do more than evaluate texts produced by others. In delineating the evolution of information literacy, Christine Pawley urged us to "recognize that information 'access' is not just about information consumerism, but also about individuals and groups of people actively shaping the world as knowledge producers in a way that renders the consumer-producer dichotomy irrelevant."[5] Similarly, James Elmborg has called attention to the meaning of literacy itself as a reflection of "the ability to read *and write*" (emphasis added).[6] Long the province of academic librarians, this philosophy can guide a broader coalition of practitioners and educators.

Given popular interest in authorship, which reflects both deeply personal and broader cultural impulses, investing time and effort in connecting with writers will bring about beneficial relationships. This shift in sensibilities is ongoing and incremental, represented in part by a smattering of articles in the professional literature that discuss how to work with self-published authors.[7] Welcoming writers to the library through informed programming and knowledgeable reference services, grounded in useful collections and information resources, is the next step. We believe that libraries can play a critical role in fostering writing in their communities, and NaNoWriMo's efforts to create partnerships with libraries is one signal of the possibilities.[8] This book is for those who want a fuller engagement with writers in their communities. In it we will look at how to communicate with would-be authors and potential programming partners, as well as what is involved in helping writers see the library as a core part of their writing experience.

Beyond explaining ways to think about what writers do and what they need when they take on specific kinds of projects, we want to give attention to the resources that can be helpful to someone who is still in the process of exploring the parameters of what they might write. Particularly when a writer says he is interested in writing a memoir or personal narrative, libraries are of value in widening the perspective and concepts that can form his story. Moreover, writers of poetry and fiction, who are more likely to see their work as imaginative rather than information-driven, can also benefit from library-based research. Because many writers want to connect with and learn from others as they struggle to shape their stories, we will also offer ideas about programming that brings individuals who are writing in a variety of traditions together at the library.

NOT MAKING THINGS UP
Research and Creation

Telling stories, whatever their origins, involves far more than imagination or invention. The classical concept of *invention* has been understood in various ways, including the "originality and independence" of an artistic creation, the "production of things 'fanciful' or incredible," pure fiction, and "the artful combination of historical truth and imaginative falsehood."[9] This long-standing discussion of creativity, however, typically ignores the role of research in creative writing. While research doesn't occupy much space in books that advise would-be writers, grappling with facts is often critical to the endeavor, though some literary critics issue cautions about the conventional limits and boundaries of realism.[10] These boundaries, of course, are always on the move. New facts erupt and a world that was flat becomes fiction. What was thought to have been overcome and left to the past, recurs. *What is there to say?* Writers keep asking that question. Librarians cannot ask it for them, but they are very well-placed to listen as more specific questions emerge that can create an image, scene, story, or book. Librarians can affirm that research is recursive but enriching, because becoming a better researcher means obtaining more options for the imagination and opening up more questions for literary exploration. In a broader sense, librarians can be there to affirm that writers' voices unfold and reveal themselves within this dynamic of balancing one's creative vision with the known world.

There are numerous examples of writers who connect imagined and real worlds, both light and dark. Authors acknowledge that the world around them factors into their fictions. Take this passage from Rainbow Rowell's *Fangirl,* a conversation between a novice writer and her creative writing professor:

> "We write about the worlds we already know. I've written four books, and they all take place within a hundred and twenty miles of my hometown. Most of them are about things that happened in my real life."
>
> "But you write historical novels—"
>
> The professor nodded. "I take something that happened to me in 1983, and I make it happen to someone else in 1943. I pick my life apart that way, try to understand it better by writing straight through it."
>
> "So everything in your books is true?"
>
> The professor tilted her head and hummed. "Mmm . . . yes. And no. Everything starts with a little truth, then I spin my

webs around it—sometimes I spin completely away from it. But the point is, I don't start with nothing."

Rowell uses this dialogue between teacher and student to illustrate what is discoverable but less acknowledged: writers depend on research as well as imagination.

Another example appears in Margaret Atwood's discussion of renewed interest in her 1985 novel, *The Handmaid's Tale*. Her book is one in which, on a profound level, nothing has actually been invented. Here's how Atwood put it in the *New York Times Book Review*:

> I'd read extensively in science fiction, speculative fiction, utopias and dystopias ever since my high school years in the 1950s, but I'd never written such a book. . . . The form was strewn with pitfalls, among them a tendency to sermonize, a veering into allegory and a lack of plausibility. If I was to create an imaginary garden I wanted the toads in it to be real. One of my rules was that I would not put any events into the book that had not already happened in what James Joyce called the "nightmare" of history, nor any technology not already available. No imaginary gizmos, no imaginary laws, no imaginary atrocities. God is in the details, they say. So is the Devil.[11]

Atwood's entire commentary on the renewed readership for her novel is worth reading, but this aspect feels particularly instructive for writers, readers, and world citizens: her novel isn't a fiction made by giving free rein to the imagination, by trying to outdistance the darkest and goriest monsters conjured up by the next writer's open-ended "what if?"—it's an assemblage of things already done, moments in the history of what we have been and, on some level, still are.

In other instances, the role of research in creating a novel or a poem is more readily evident. Critics noted that Curtis Sittenfeld's *American Wife* (2008), a fictionalized account of a First Lady's life modeled on Laura Bush, at times hews rather closely to Bush's lived and documented experience. Particularly in the matter of a car accident that resulted in another driver's death, one reviewer observed, "Questioned about this incident by journalists, Alice Blackwell repeats verbatim the carefully chosen words in which Laura Bush replies when confronted with similar questions."[12] In other words, Sittenfeld didn't invent the difficult dialogue; she researched it. Locating those words involved the use of databases and search strategies, expert knowledge, and evaluation of the records that represented the First Lady's history in news articles and other documents. In a similar vein, scholars and writers alike have observed Walt Whitman's inclusion of scientific discoveries in his poems as evidence that he, too, relied on research in creating his account of American life in the nineteenth century. Elsewhere, this has been described as the difference between the imperative to "write what you know" and the ability to "write what you can find out."[13]

Increasingly, contemporary authors acknowledge this tension between knowledge and imagination. Prior to the publication of her novel *Commonwealth* (2016), Ann Patchett expressed concerns about its reception—specifically where critics would place their focus: "I have a real fear that the whole publication of this novel is going to center around questions of autobiography, which isn't nearly as interesting as whether or not the novel is any good." Patchett openly acknowledged that "I certainly drew from things that were much closer to my life" in the new book, but she noted that her previous fiction had always been "about my family, but up until now I'd been very clever to hide everyone in giant costumes of chicken wire and masking tape."[14] Her worries were not entirely unfounded. Readers have long found parallels between a writer's life and work intriguing, and many professional critics and others find it possible to consider these echoes within the larger question of whether or not a book is any good. The exposure of the identity of the pseudonymous novelist Elena Ferrante and subsequent criticisms of her fiction focused on correlations between lived experience and the printed page highlights the dogged, even unkind, pursuit of these questions of truth and authenticity.[15] Perhaps these authors' books, with their rave reviews and readerly affection, provide an object lesson in how knowledge drawn from the past can be reworked into a vividly contoured act of storytelling that is not strictly tethered to the facts of people, places, and events.[16]

Accordingly, this book offers a broad, conceptual reconsideration of what a library can be, as well as offering specific sorts of projects and prompts that can be offered to library users. We hope, ultimately, to reach individuals operating in different settings, and so we talk about what creative writing in libraries can do in very general ways, juxtaposed with examples of what this type of professional work looks like on the ground.

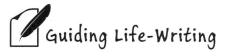 Guiding Life-Writing

Some of us want, first and foremost, to write about ourselves. This is an individual endeavor, but it is not necessarily solipsistic or myopic. Beyond self-expression, this sort of narrative has the potential to engage with and add to the community's sense of itself by capturing part of its history through an individual's story—was she the first woman to hold a municipal office, or did she live through a distinctive time period, like the civil rights protests of the 1960s?—and we can encourage the writer to use the library's resources to refine and elaborate on her narrative. Whether by housing the resulting text or supporting its development, we can aid writers and their communities who want to tell their own stories in an encompassing way.

Such writing might align with several different genres, such as oral history, autobiography, or memoir. It might also fall into the category of a personal essay or a family profile. Walt Whitman's famous line, "I celebrate myself and sing myself," may be seen as warranting a long tradition of using verse to explain or justify oneself; more recently, in the twentieth century, a school of poets created what came to be known as confessional poetry or "poetry of the personal or 'I.'"[17] The author Maggie Nelson, among others, uses the phrase "life-writing" to describe works that adopt the aim of telling a personal story while adapting linguistic, cultural, and narrative conventions to one's own ends.[18] Regardless of the label, many individuals are invested in finding ways to tell their own stories.

One challenge may be getting people who are genuinely enthusiastic about telling their own stories to expand their scope a bit. Librarians looking for ways to encourage storytelling and self-reflection, relying on memory and research alike, can encourage patrons to use library resources to situate their individual experiences in a wider context. Research generates new perspectives and questions that can allow them to grow their writing into something more dynamic, complicated, and compelling through activities and discussion.

Focusing on the pathway between these two places, between *my* story and a larger, impersonal one that unfolds with the assistance of an archive or a library, isn't actually all that difficult to undertake within the act of writing. No writer steps out of history and simply begins telling a fully independent story. What's more, an author who proceeds with a greater degree of care and urgency in naming the when and where that a story begins in often does so precisely because the broader circumstances surrounding this telling are so uncertain, verging on the chaotic, as they press in on the memory and the writing simultaneously. The opening three sentences of James Baldwin's essay "Notes of a Native Son" provide a powerful example: "On the twenty-ninth of July, in 1943, my father died. On the same day, a few hours later, his last child was born. Over a month before this, while all our energies were concentrated on waiting for these events, there had been, in Detroit, one of the bloodiest race riots of the century."[19] The scaffold of Baldwin's entire narrative is largely contained in these initial gestures, though the undertaking of his essay, which is arguably the greatest of the twentieth century, is to make sense of these intersections. In order to say what happened to his family, to his country, and to himself, he will not create a bird's-eye view of events or attempt to separate the personal and political but will let their entanglement frame his agonized meditation. While no one else can be James Baldwin, the point of personal narratives of any stripe is that they provide a lens onto the times and places they are describing. This is part of what libraries support. "You think your pain and heartbreak are unprecedented in the history of the world," Baldwin told an interviewer in 1963, "then you read."[20]

Librarians often begin their analysis of narratives in a comparable way, leading discussions for One Community, One Book events and other library-based reading groups. To move from reading and discussion into research-based writing related to the self, librarians could draw on the following short prompts to guide writers in exploring information that would contribute to their life stories:

> Using a database to look into what else was happening in the world the day, week, or month that patrons were born. If your library has a popular EBSCO suite of research databases, you will first need patrons to switch from the basic to the advanced search mode. There it is possible to search for the month of one's birth only by setting both

month-year fields to the appropriate month and year within the Published Date field under Limit Your Results.

Directing participants to write their clearest, most detailed memory of an event from their life that other people witnessed. This could form the core of one in-library writing activity, with writers sharing passages from their work with one another. They would later, on their own, call one or more of the people whom they remember at this event in order to see how they remember the event.

Participants could be asked to write about a very public event or a cultural artifact that had a particular resonance for them and was bound into the fabric of their life narratives. This prompt could be used in numerous ways. For example, if the library holds artifacts or is hosting a display of artifacts, these items could serve as the basis for the exercise. Otherwise, participants can be asked to select their own event or artifact. As with the earlier prompt, you can ask people to write, allowing them to grapple for details, before turning to databases (whether a general, licensed resource or a more specifically applicable one), in order to compare and contrast their memories with documentary sources.

Essentially, the goal of these questions is to encourage a moment of double-exposure, creating a multiplicity of perspectives as a guide for literary composition. Archives and other sources can offer memory aids; importantly, they can tell us things we don't know about our own past, which actually belong to us as much as the things we feel capable of narrating without any help.

TRUTH, VERISIMILITUDE, AND VOICES FROM THE ARCHIVES

Anyone working with writers is likely to encounter both those who believe, unflinchingly, in the possibility of finding and representing truth, as well as those who bring the skepticism of the academy to this notion. The question we are considering is, in essence, this: if we are teaching patrons to do research, are we insisting that they must engage in realism as a literary mode or in personal truth-telling as a writing objective? The answer is both simple and complicated.

The question of truth and the related concept of verisimilitude have long literary histories that we'll explore briefly as a means of describing the centrality of these concerns to practicing, publishing writers. In short, our aim is to keep an earnest and well-meaning librarian from being blindsided by a potentially acrimonious debate through awareness of the differing schools of thought on truth, verisimilitude, and the resulting work with archival and primary source materials.

The question of truth and artistry emerges often in nonfiction and especially in what is referred to as creative nonfiction, where what's presumed to be creative is the fact-bending and distortions of the historical record. John D'Agata, the coauthor of *The Lifespan of a Fact* (2012), has become the most visible representative of a position maintaining that the term *nonfiction* is a misnomer, a fundamentally negative definition that doesn't tell you what a genre actually is, merely what it isn't. In place of this negation he has proposed, primarily over the course of multiple anthologies, a many-sided understanding of the essay as a form of art. The strictures of documented or knowable truth are secondary to its primary obligation, which is to extend the oldest sense of the term *essay*—an attempt, an experiment, a trying-out—into new territory. D'Agata's earliest proposals for this more hybridized work, drawing from fact, fiction, and poetics, were associated with what was termed the lyric essay, a concept that has continued to meet resistance and skepticism. That said, creative nonfiction also often functions more like a brand than a concept or object with clear outlines. The term *creative nonfiction* has a long-standing association with the teaching and editorial work of Lee Gutkind and is literally attached to a journal of that name which he founded in 1993, alongside the credo that "You can't make this stuff up." This is a sharp and recognizable catchphrase, but it leaves complex questions about human memory and historiography largely untouched.

While the breadth and flexibility of nonfiction are among its many virtues, the separate, overlapping traditions within it do not always tolerate the sorts of liberties with documented truth that D'Agata has endorsed. Recurring outrages over work published as autobiography that turns out to be exaggerated or fabricated is the most obvious example. Few writers hope to become the next James Frey, though it should be noted that the royalties retained from his book did allow him to accumulate a significant personal collection of contemporary art. The shared crisis of civic (mis)understanding and anxiety around the status and legitimacy of facts in the "post-truth" era only serves to highlight and exaggerate these long-simmering tensions: it does not "prove" that it is time for lyric essayists to stop smudging the boundaries between genres any more than it confirms that investigative journalism is interchangeable with hallucinating. Verifiability and consensus are part of the picture, but so are contested imaginings of what information even *is* and how it should be treated. These are broad, thorny issues extending unevenly across the field of nonfiction, but autobiography particularizes them in ways that are both useful and limited.

Mary Karr, the author of three memoirs and a critical guide to that form, has offered comparatively straightforward directions for aspiring memoirists for whom vetting sources is a primary concern. First and foremost is the act of trying to write down one's memories with as much detail and life as possible. Then the writer asks others who were present at any of the incidents how, or even if, they remember them. Karr's own practice is to note in passing when the recollections of others differ from her own, but this is a qualification rather than an automatic grounds for dismissal. While it might be observed that writers like Gutkind are essentially trying to do story-based journalism with a strong personal angle, Karr pictures this search for veracity as inseparable from the attempt of the memoirist to render a life. "Truth is not their *enemy*. It's the bannister they grab for when feeling around on the dark cellar stairs. It's the solution."[21] It likely comes as no surprise that these writers have their analogues among academic historians and individuals interested in historiography. Roger Chartier has emerged as a staunch defender of telling historical stories with as much allegiance as possible to what he calls the voices in the archives; he contrasts his stance with that of critics like Hayden White, who sees historical works as essentially narratives that are constructed and plotted in much the same way that fiction is.[22]

Another related consideration is verisimilitude in fiction. Anyone who has participated in a discussion of a novel set in a familiar city has likely heard someone insist that a detail in the book is not the way it is in real life, that the building isn't where the author put it, so the action that follows isn't possible, and so on. While writers have to make their own decisions about the extent to which they wish to be true to facts, based on their personal ideals and the nature of their project, the library has many resources that allow people to engage this issue in nonconfrontational ways. One example of the modification of historical reality can be found in the director's cut of the film adaptation of Michael Cunningham's *The Hours,* when Nicole Kidman talks about her portrayal of Virginia Woolf. Kidman listened to the few extant recordings of Woolf's voice but observes that the voice isn't what contemporary Americans expect an Englishwoman from an earlier era to sound like, so there's divergence between how she played the character and what the real person represented by the character sounded like. In this case, the decision was to create an effect, rather than replicating what was. While we don't want to make those decisions for novice writers, in what follows we supply resources that show how creators with experience make these judgment calls.

Finally, there is the concept of poetic license, which originated as a way of describing poets' prerogative of deviating from formal elements of verse and now refers, more colloquially, to someone's deviation from facts for effect. (This principle is central to a hilariously credible story that John Green tells about learning to tell stories while at Kenyon College.)[23] At the same time that there is a core definition of the concept of poetic license, different writers have offered significantly varying takes on it. Their voices reveal that writers think about these things, set up rules for themselves, and pursue relationships to the truth that they are trying to make resonate on the page. For some, this might be above all an emotional truth that is going to happen because we feel like we're in the presence of a human being we could never otherwise know, one who has been created, essentially, through fiction. On the other hand, there are people who can work, in extraordinarily creative and imaginative ways, with an absolute devotion to not saying anything they cannot prove, that wasn't said, observed, reported in peer-reviewed journals, and so on. John McPhee, who has been awarded the Pulitzer Prize for nonfiction, has adamantly affirmed this philosophy, exemplified by the title of his recurring course at Princeton: "The Literature of Fact."

Librarians need an awareness of these different schools of thought and work; they need not take sides, but they should be equipped to offer options in response to the demands that different aspiring authors will make of them. This pertains both to questions that individuals might ask and the possibilities for library-based writing programs.

For instance, we might encourage a writing exercise in which authors commit to writing a piece in which they are devoted, in a pinky-swear kind of way, to telling nothing but the truth. Alternatively, writers could be given a prompt to write three separate scenes: two of them factual, one fictional. Their peers can guess which is which, and the writer may feel better informed about how and when he created a piece of language that felt particularly authentic for an audience. Furthermore, librarians can present the tools for learning or backing up the claims to the truth as a writer knows it. There are many ways to do this: instruction in using library resources and acts like citing and triangulating sources; locating specific information, such as eyewitness accounts of historical details; or dealing with writers' queries about how to confirm that this building was built on that street, that people in the country where they've set their story had access to dogs of that particular breed, and so on. Additionally, librarians can host a discussion, perhaps with an invited author from the community, that addresses how and why it is fun to write a piece that starts with research (in order to find out what you don't know and maybe can't know, or in order to tweak it for a particular reason), and then build on that in a variety of ways. Discussions of these prompts, in the end, reveal why contortions of fact can be just as (or even more) interesting than making things up out of thin air, but they require writers to know something in order to twist it and show another angle or unexpected detail.

CONCLUSION

One strategy we will use in the chapters ahead is to show how a particular work pulls off a particular effect and then discuss how librarians can connect that to a prompt or exercise in order to anchor a creative writing program in your library. We'll do this even though it might be more useful, at least initially, for you to simply offer a well-known book—maybe a Community Reads title—as a starting point and build from there, using whatever momentum or interest the book created to lead to the next thing—signing folks up for your program or getting prompts out to the patrons who responded strongly to that book.

We're hoping to offer strategies for thinking about how to lasso a general enthusiasm for literature and direct it toward creative writing and the research that strengthens it, but doing this means making an effort to create another option within the library space. For those who see creative writing as a nice extra that competes for a library's limited time and staff, we will offer guidelines to help facilitate how libraries can reach out to writers and teachers in the community, potential partners who might volunteer to support this type of programming. We want to map out how writing gets connected to research, so we show you how those volunteers can collaborate with the library and incorporate elements into programs that will help would-be writers to become better at gathering information, not just competent storytellers or sonnet-makers.

Following this introduction to the idea of libraries, archives, and databases as supports for various sorts of creative writing, using finding aids and other search principles form a final chapter, along with guidance on using interviews as part of the research process. The tools that librarians have long used to answer homework questions, to help entrepreneurs, to satisfy a patron's curiosity, and more are all tools that writers can use to build characters, envision worlds, and create the stories that form in their imaginations.

Notes

1. Timothy Kim, "National Novel Writing Month Blasts Off on a Literary Adventure" (press release), October 25, 2016.

2. Samantha Raphelson, "Iraqi Refugee Empowers Youth to Share Their Stories," NPR (May 25, 2017), www.npr.org/2017/05/25/530074663/iraqi -refugee-empowers-youth-to-share-their-stories-with-narration.

3. "Cumulative Total of Tumblr Blogs 2011–2018," Statistica: The Statistics Portal (n.d.), https://www.statista.com/statistics/256235/total-cumulative -number-of-tumblr-blogs/.

4. John Mutter, "LBF 2017: 'Pretty Good Year' for Booksellers," Shelf Awareness (March 17, 2017), www.shelf-awareness.com/issue.html?issue =2959#m35814.

5. Christine Pawley, "Information Literacy: A Contradictory Coupling," *The Library Quarterly* 73, no. 422 :(2003) 4–52.

6. James K. Elmborg, "Critical Information Literacy: Definitions and Challenges," *Transforming Information Literacy Programs: Intersecting Frontiers of Self, Library Culture, and Campus Community* 78 :(2012) 64.

7. These articles often debate cataloging practices and argue the importance of getting past a reticence in dealing with authors who lack the imprimatur of a major press; see, for example, James LaRue, "No Cold Shoulder in Kentucky: Self-Publishing & Libraries," *Library Journal* (September 4, 2015), http:// lj.libraryjournal.com/2015/09/publishing/self-publishing-and-libraries/ no-cold-shoulder-in-kentucky-self-publishing-libraries/.

8. "Come Write In," NaNoWriMo, http://nanowrimo.org/come-write-in.

9. Alex Preminger, Frank J. Warnke, and Osborne Bennett Hardison Jr., eds., *Princeton Encyclopedia of Poetry and Poetics* (Princeton, NJ: Princeton University Press, 2015), 628.

10. Erich Auerbach, *Mimesis: The Representation of Reality in Western Literature,* trans. Willard R. Trask (Princeton, NJ: Princeton University Press, 1971), 31.

11. Margaret Atwood, "Margaret Atwood on What 'The Handmaid's Tale' Means in the Age of Trump," *New York Times Book Review* (March 2017 ,10), 14–15.

12. Joyce Carol Oates, "The First Lady," *New York Times Book Review* (August 29, 2008), www.nytimes.com/2008/08/31/books/review/Oates-t.html.

13. Megan Marshall, "Show *and* Tell," Letters to the Editor, *New York Times Book Review* (May 19, 2017), https://www.nytimes.com/2017/05/19/books/review/ letters-to-the-editor.html.

14. "'None of It Happened and All of It's True'—Ann Patchett's *Commonwealth,*" Musing, https://parnassusmusing.net/2016/08/29/none-of-it-happened-and -all-of-its-true-ann-patchett-on-her-new-novel-commonwealth/.

15. Alexandra Schwarts, "The 'Unmasking' of Elena Ferrante," *The New Yorker* (October 3, 2016), https://www.newyorker.com/culture/cultural-comment/ the-unmasking-of-elena-ferrante.

16. This idea is discussed in a compilation created by Emily Temple, "Should You Write What You Know? 31 Authors Weigh In," Lit Hub (February 7,

2018), https://lithub.com/should-you-write-what-you-know-31-authors
-weigh-in/.

17. "A Brief Guide to Confessional Poetry," Poetry Foundation, https://www
.poets.org/poetsorg/text/brief-guide-confessional-poetry.

18. "I'm interested in the kind of life-writing that's inexhaustible, i.e., that has
little to do with the 'summing up' typically indicated by the word 'memoir'"
as Nelson explained in a 2016 interview, "Sasha Frere-Jones and Maggie
Nelson discuss writing and form," *Los Angeles Times* (March 8, 2016), https://
www.latimes.com/books/jacketcopy/la-et-jc-sasha-frere-jones-maggie
-nelson-q-a-20160307-story.html.

19. Phillip Lopate, ed., *The Art of the Personal Essay: An Anthology from the
Classical Era to the Present* (Anchor, 1995), 587.

20. Jane Howard, "Telling Talk from a Negro Writer," *LIFE Magazine* 54, no. 21
(May 24, 1963): 63.

21. Mary Karr, *The Art of Memoir* (New York: HarperCollins, 2015).

22. Hayden White, *The Content of the Form: Narrative Discourse and Historical
Representation* (Baltimore, MD: Johns Hopkins University Press, 2009).

23. Kenyon College, "John Green—Thoughts on How to Make Things
and Why" (February 13, 2014), YouTube, https://www.youtube.com/
watch?v=R4peoHkXsJg.

1

All Past Years

Historical writing might be described as an account of the past, but even a little prodding unearths divergent ideas about what history ought to be. You will find, quite quickly, that writers have different ideas about when something becomes historical and what should be preserved, or revealed, with words. That something that took place a hundred years ago is a historical event is unlikely to be disputed; however, attitudes toward something that happened yesterday might be more contentious. What if yesterday is August 5, 2018? What if yesterday is August 5, 2018, and you live in Bali? What if yesterday is November 8, 2016? What if yesterday is November 22, 1963? As David M. Kennedy has written, "We all live in history. Some of us make it, others are made—or broken— by it."[1] Subscribing to the idea that only a handful of figures truly "make" history, while the rest of us are passive receivers of it, is a limited and outdated conception of the word *history*. By considering history as more than the passage of time, as something inflected by place and person, we can begin to consider how different narratives about the past emerge, and we can take into account the different materials that a writer might draw on in the retelling of history. John Donne's persona challenges his interlocutor to "tell me where all past years are," though he is all too intentionally aware of the impossibility of this request. There are, then, necessary limits to this discussion of a wide-ranging subject.

Before closing off directions, it is useful to acknowledge the varied terrain of historical writing. Although it may be conventional to think of historical writing as nonfiction narrative, history encompasses many genres. Hayden White, for example, distinguishes between chronology, or lists ordered by date, and structures with more readily discernible, narrative organizing principles. In *A History of Histories* (2007), John Burrow constructs a longer list of historical genres, noting the use of some that we now regard as fiction, like epic and myth, which are consequently less important to knowledge than they were in earlier eras. Modes of telling, too, can vary considerably, and they are a factor in the finished works available to readers. In this chapter, a discussion of prose works and research resources precedes our attention to documentary poetry, a verse form most strongly associated with alternative voices on historical incidents. Through these topics, we hope to illuminate the different types of historical writing that library users may be interested in.

The relationship between the present and the past, and how it serves to focus our attention on particular historical moments and actors, often motivates writers' research on historical subjects. In *Telling the Truth about History* (1994), Joyce Appleby and her coauthors observe: "What historians do best is to make connections with the past in order to illuminate the problems of the present and the potential of the future."[2] Although scholarship and secondary sources are valuable to a writer's knowledge, aiding in the creation of perspective and interpretation, primary sources are integral to developing a sense of the past. This chapter focuses on some of the more general resources that serve these purposes and discusses strategies of interpretation that enable writers to make the best use of documents that might reflect different linguistic and cultural norms.

Appleby and her coauthors observe that "in the seventeenth and eighteenth centuries" people in Europe "began to develop . . . an appreciation of how the passage of time changes institutions

TO READ MORE ABOUT DOING HISTORY, SEE:

- Joyce Appleby, Lynn Hunt, and Margaret Jacob, *Telling the Truth about History* (New York: W.W. Norton, 1994), for how a sense of history defines a nation and changes people's sense of who they are and where they come from.

- *A Little History of* Series (Yale University Press) for short, accessible narratives of different subjects inspired by Ernst Gombrich's *A Little History of the World* (1935).

- Margaret MacMillan, *Dangerous Games: The Uses and Abuses of History* (Modern Library, 2009), for a critique of the popularization of historical forms to serve political ends, written by a major U.S. scholar.

- Louise Robbins, *The Dismissal of Miss Ruth Brown* (University of Oklahoma Press, 2000), the story of a librarian fired for her efforts to desegregate an Oklahoma public library during the McCarthy era, which includes grounded discussions of the author's research strategies.

and renders past societies strikingly different from contemporary ones." This intellectual phenomenon, which they label *historical consciousness,* is something we might regard as crucial to the act of writing history.[3] Seeing the past as different from the present because of the accumulation of knowledge or shifting cultural values sometimes drives historical work; conversely, historians have found stories that, despite the remoteness of time or place, resonate with familiar feelings. In our era, with people calling attention to instances of injustice and long-accepted language that is riddled with bias, the tensions between the truth found in artifacts and documents from days gone by and our current perceptions of their significance may require persistence and openness in order to reconcile them. Historians such as Roger Chartier and Natalie Zemon Davis encourage us to diligently follow evidentiary paths in order to enhance and correct our understanding of events that we cannot know firsthand, while recognizing the limits of language and seeing power in reviving once-suppressed stories.

The tools that historians employ in these endeavors have been sequestered in chilly institutional archives, saved as microfilm in endless rows of metal cabinets, or tucked away in overheated home attics. Boxes with personal papers, packed away and all but forgotten, represent a mythic image of what historians hope to find in the process of their research. The reality, particularly in the twenty-first century, is both more prosaic and more dynamic.

Newspapers claim the role of creating the rough draft of history. These days, some have suggested, perhaps in jest, that Twitter and other social media platforms contain the initial versions of our collective story. As more people obtain their news from online outlets, whether first-person pronouncements or the vetted work of newspapers of record, more of the so-called "rough drafts" of history can be found on particular platforms and websites. Smaller newspapers that record the nature of life far from the nation's capital and centers of commerce, unfortunately, may be slower in shifting to online publishing. As a consequence, searches of a newspaper's "morgue," as the in-house, print repository of previous editions is known among journalists, or a for-fee database like LexisNexis, may be the only avenues of access to these publications.

Other resources will provide data that require more interpretation and effort to align the details they provide against material from other sources. One intriguing source of historical information is the census. The census operates at both federal and state levels, and the questions asked on its forms can vary considerably. Those same forms, their language and priorities, also offer a window onto the concerns of the time. Data collected may include only basics such as an individual's name and family members, ages, occupations and incomes, along with where they lived. Some census forms, however, were intended to gather far more information, like literacy, race, disabilities, and so on. One Iowa census sought to aggregate the proportion of the state's residents employed in agricultural occupations versus other settings, how many owned homes rather than rented, which wars people were veterans of, and more. Because the forms were completed by census takers who went door to door, using this information depends on reading cursive as well as being able to locate an individual in the records.

City directories and Sanborn maps are other tools that can help writers learn about a neighborhood or a city as it once existed, whether they want to locate an old family home or learn about where a famous person came from. Directories provide details like addresses and, eventually, phone numbers. Sanborn Fire Insurance Maps, initially developed to allow underwriters to assess risk, now allow authors to see the physical layout of a place, the proximity of neighbors, and the rate at which a neighborhood grew. Beginning in 1866 and continuing into the present, the Sanborn company mapped tens of thousands of U.S. cities.[4] ProQuest maintains a database of Sanborn maps from 1867 to 1970, if your library contracts for access. Because institutions are aware of the cost of these digitized resources, some of them have sought grant funding and other support to make older Sanborn maps available, though often with limited searchability:

- The Library of Congress has digitized thousands of older Sanborn maps, and other entities also provide regional access.[5]
- Michigan State University has an all-encompassing finding aid, providing links to the online map collections in many states.[6]
- Indiana University has tried to locate and list the sources for all the Indiana maps dating to 1923, which are no longer protected by copyright.[7]
- The Earth Sciences and Map Library at UC Berkeley has a dedicated web page, which includes links to digitized maps, organized by state, complemented by a bibliography of research on Sanborn maps to help users understand these historical documents.[8]

Writers who wonder about what a city used to look like, then, have an opportunity to envision it based on more than just surviving photos and verbal descriptions.

If a writer approaches you with questions about whether someone's personal papers still exist, one tool that may provide answers is the National Union Catalog of Manuscript Collections (NUCMC).[9] Optimal search strategies will vary with changes to this database, which is maintained by the Library of Congress, so you will want to consult the NUCMC website for advice on its use. This resource has the potential, though, to help users determine where someone's papers are held and how extensive the surviving materials may be. It might be best to think of this as a first step, rather than an exhaustive one, in locating personal papers and archival materials. Finding aids and access policies at the institution that owns the sought-after materials, for example, are a necessary complement to NUCMC records. Digitization projects, for-fee services, and freelance researchers may provide alternatives to self-funded travel to far-flung collections; moreover, a small number of major research libraries offer competitive funding to help researchers defray the costs of traveling to use their distinctive holdings.

Other online tools may also prove useful for this type of information-seeking. The American Philosophical Society website, for example, has an extensive guide to diaries in its collection, including a discussion of diaries as primary sources and how the guide's more than 400 subject terms were created.[10] It is worth remembering, too, that some letters and diaries have been published, providing access to their words outside the archives. Projects like the decade-long Navajo Oral History Project, whose videos can be located by searching that phrase rather than via a central site or YouTube channel, represent another way that first-person testimonials may be found. Transcriptions of an earlier Navajo oral history project are available, too, via the University of New Mexico.[11]

As special libraries and archives increase their outreach through social media, it is possible that users might find images and descriptions through platforms like Twitter and Tumblr. The vogue for particular hashtags ebbs and fades, but they remain potentially searchable. Suggestions for finding these institutions, collectively, involve the broad terms *special collections* and *archives,* regardless of platform. Twitter users are prone to variant forms, like the shorthand *speccoll, SpColl,* and so on. These organizations may use thematic hashtags, like #bookfrights at Halloween, to highlight seasonally appropriate holdings. Locating a particular archive on a specific platform and reading its recent posts for hashtags can also enable you to follow a focused dialogue across institutions that hold useful and unique materials.

Questions about historical detail may, at first glance, seem daunting. What did people eat during the Middle Ages? How would someone buy a book in eighteenth-century France? What was a common cause of death in Victorian London? Are there guides to Native American trails? Because the resources that help users visualize earlier eras aren't always part of a nonspecialist's repertoire or a library's catalog, we want to highlight some of the documents that serve writers' desires for insights into the past. An array of historical research sources are collected in a PDF from the "Write Your Own Hamilton" talk at NerdCon (https://ir.uiowa.edu/slis _pubs/16/), and the materials below are signposts to the historical material in that document and elsewhere:[12]

> College yearbooks indicate something about gender balance in enrollments, as well as clothing and hairstyles; they will also suggest something about hobbies and leisure activities, and what was considered amusing to that generation. Advertisements also often serve as cultural barometers, and Duke University has a sizable digital collection (https://library.duke .edu/digitalcollections/advertising/).[13]
>
> Every celebrity and royal baby seems to focus attention on naming trends; the Social Security Administration maintains lists of popular baby names going back to the 1880s (https://www.ssa .gov/oact/babynames/), and search tools enable users to see the geographic distribution of name trends, too.[14]
>
> Brown University's John Hay Library maintains a sword collection, as well as other significant military history materials.[15]
>
> Genealogical resources are useful beyond that specialization, and Ft. Wayne's Allen County Public Library Genealogy Center (www.genealogycenter.org/) is one of the foremost outlets in this area.[16]
>
> African-American migration patterns within the United States are discussed and mapped in conjunction with the art of Jacob Lawrence.[17] Libraries are also developing collections

to tell the story of the fight for civil rights, such as the Civil Rights Digital Library, among others, and collections recognizing LGBTQ individuals and issues, as at the New York Public Library.[18]

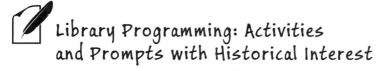

Library Programming: Activities and Prompts with Historical Interest

▨ Ransom Riggs has explained the genesis of *Miss Peregrine's Home for Peculiar Children* (2011) in oddly compelling old photos, some of which seem to show things that defy ready explanation.[19] What photos can you find, perhaps in your library's local history holdings or old copies of the local newspaper, that might provide similar prompts? Digitizing a few of these images could serve as a visual prompt in which writers create explanations for what they see in those photographs.

▨ Lawrence Sutin's *A Postcard Memoir* (2003) begins with a similar personal archive of images—his collection of antique postcards—though the text that these generate is autobiographical rather than fictional. Depending on their interests and sensibility, some writers may feel more drawn to the challenge of elaborating the memories evoked by images rather than building a fictional world.

▨ In our own practice, we have used a short passage from a historical novel as a prompt for a brief discussion. By presenting a group with a readable (i.e., not too long, not too dense) excerpt from a work that takes place in a different era and giving members time to peruse it, you can host a discussion. Essentially, you are asking writers to identify and evaluate the details that give a sense of the historical period, considering how those details make the differences in that period vivid and real. While we did this as a preliminary to information-sharing, it would be possible to provide a set of examples from writers who use different strategies, in a sort of compare-and-contrast exercise. In selecting your examples for discussion, bear in mind what Chimamanda Ngozi Adichie called "the danger of a single story" or a univalent sense of history, and seek diverse voices; examples that are closely aligned will likely prove antithetical to a more robust discussion of different storytelling techniques.[20]

▨ On Twitter, Boston-based author Rick Riordan challenged writers with this "story starter idea": "At Harvard, deep in the library archives, there are 'Z cabinets' which contain items too big for normal shelving, such as T. S. Eliot's hat. Sometimes forgotten relics, manuscripts, etc., are unearthed in them. Go!"[21] His idea is one that can be employed in any library, either in its original form or with examples of oddities in more local collections.

▨ Libraries, in addition to containing history books, have histories of their own. Are there historical elements of your library available for writers to examine and evaluate for what they might reveal about the library's origins? Different types of artifacts—old shelf lists, early titles still in the collection, previous policy statements, decorative elements retained despite expansion and building rehabilitation—could yield different impressions and ideas about your institution's past. ✒

Our focus has been on the documents and resources involved in writing history, understood, as John Burrow has written, as "elaborated, secular prose narratives of public events, based on inquiry," but research underpins historical fiction as well, or even historical elements of other fictional genres. Within *Harry Potter and the Sorcerer's Stone* there is a mention of one Nicolas Flamel, who actually lived in fourteenth-century France and became an apocryphal figure after his death. While his tombstone now is protected within the walls of the Musée de Cluny, it is one of the documents reproduced within the pages of *Harry Potter: A History of Magic* (2017), and a digital page on the Pottermore site offers J. K. Rowling's testimonial to its role in creating this character. A book like Kate Milford's *Left-Handed Fate* (2016), set in eighteenth-century America, is imbued with period detail, from sailors' superstitions to unpaved streets and gas lamps, to the ways news was made public. Finding facts from the past may serve many writers, even those who want to do something other than a conventional history.

Engaging with history is not exclusively the province of prose writers but of poets as well, especially since storytelling, which shares its root word, *story*, with history, has a longer history among poets than among novelists. Epic poets like Homer and Virgil sang of the rise and fall of heroes and nations; Old Norse *skalds* recited courtly verse on historical themes; and the Old English figures of *scops* are said to have propagated the myths and legends that sometimes served as history among early Anglo-Saxon cultures. While such poets' engagements with history tended more toward myth than historical authenticity, their authorship still relied on the "historical" accounts that preceded their own.

An epic poem is a long narrative poem about heroic or extraordinary deeds and events in the past. Today, the epic poem has evolved into forms Homer would find unrecognizable, but many of its features that draw from history persist. One formal feature of the epic poem, for instance, is the Catalogue of Ships. In Homer's *Iliad* the Catalogue of Ships was an enumeration of the various factions of the Greek army that sailed to make war on Troy. In Juliana Spahr's collection *this connection of everyone with lungs* (2004), an epic-poetic meditation on the aftermath of the U.S. invasion of Iraq in 2003, she lists the weapons used by the United States to wage its campaign. She and other more recent poets have largely ignored or subverted other conventions of the epic poem. Seldom do modern and contemporary poets begin a poem by invoking the muses, stating a theme, or beginning in the middle of a great war (as the *Iliad* does). Indeed, by 1934, Ezra Pound declared an epic merely to be "a poem containing history."[22] Although more recent poets may no longer be interested in all the formal conventions of Homeric verse, they have remained attentive, as Homer was, to history itself.

Writing a Contemporary Epic

This activity enables participants to write a historical poem, one that tells a hero's story, and it is an opportunity to send your participants into the stacks. Alternately, you could select nonfiction titles and biographies for your participants to use as source material, emphasizing recent events or local heroes. These activities form a sequence of activities that can be done over the course of multiple meetings, since some of these activities are more involved, or more time-intensive, than others.

▓ Review and discuss the features of an epic poem, which you can find defined at the Poetry Foundation's "Glossary" or in volumes like the *Princeton Encyclopedia of Poetry and Poetics,* which might be on the library's shelves.[23] Issues to take up with the writers who have gathered include the following topics and questions:

◎ An epic poem is typically the story, told in verse, of a hero's journey. In its conventional form, it was a long narrative. Ask your participants to discuss who is considered a hero today and why.

◎ An epic poem might begin by drawing on the long-standing convention of stating a theme. Participants could list topics or themes of interest as a prelude to choosing a subject for their epic.

▓ As a group, read Henry Wadsworth Longfellow's "Paul Revere's Ride," which can be found on the Web, as a prelude to discussion.[24] The virtues of this poem include its relative brevity and familiarity, features which facilitate its use in this type of setting.

◎ Typically, the epic narrative begins in the middle of the action rather than at the beginning. Much of the narrative of Longfellow's "Paul Revere" has already happened before the second stanza. Where the action begins and what we read as a result merits discussion.

◎ The epic usually contains a list or enumeration of some sort, traditionally of soldiers or arms, as in Homer. Longfellow's poem alludes to the traditional Catalogue of Ships with his description of the British man-of-war Somerset in the third stanza, to which he devotes several lines.

▓ Encourage participants to write short epic poems of their own, either working with or playing against its conventions. Historically, epics have been about "great men." So your participants might write epics about notable women, whether Ruby Bridges or Ruth Bader Ginsburg. In place of a catalog or list of armaments intended for battle, writers might enumerate a more figurative arsenal possessed by the poem's subject.

▓ Writers may find reference consultations helpful, once they have settled on their subject(s).

▓ Follow up by providing time and space for participants to share their writing. ✒

Where Percy Shelley once proclaimed poets "the unacknowledged legislators of the world," documentary poets have become the unacknowledged historians, since they strive to witness, document, and in many cases, revise historical accounts. They employ poetics as a form of social and political activism. These poets often amend official histories or historical records to include victims and marginalized voices. For example, Carolyn Forché wrote her most famous poem, "The Colonel," about her work as a human rights activist in Central America during the Salvadoran Civil War, when violent political regimes silenced their civilian opponents by death squads. Muriel Rukeyser included subjects who were illiterate, as well as those who had died before the publication of her book, *U.S. 1* (1938). These and other examples allow us to consider how librarians and educators might make use of subsequent conventions and forms as an opportunity for research and dialogue.

We see poetry limning social conditions—a nexus of labor, empire, history, and race—when, in 1925, a young Langston Hughes pondered poetry's relationship to history and social justice in a short meditation on colonialism called "Johannesburg Mines":

> In the Johannesburg mines
> There are 240,000
> Native Africans working.
> What kind of poem
> Would you
> Make out of that?
> 240,000 natives
> Working in the
> Johannesburg mines.

Hughes sets the "240,000 / Native" African laborers against the colonial name of the municipality that marks the mines, which he repeats to envelop his nine-line poem. Hughes is clearly attentive to the politics and histories of colonization that have resulted in the situation, but his speaker also asks what to do with that attention in the name of poetry: "What kind of poem / Would you / Make out of that?"

Many writers can be understood as responding to Hughes's question, generating both literary theory and verse. Authors of documentary poetry craft work that is sometimes distinct from, and in other cases, aligned with the politically sympathetic "poetry of witness." Carolyn Forché advanced our sense of a "poetry of witness" through two influential anthologies, *Poetry of Witness: The Tradition in English, 1500–2001* (2014) and *Against Forgetting: Twentieth-Century Poetry of Witness* (1993). The former collection focuses on Anglophone poets' concerns with how history has been written since at least the sixteenth century and how it continues amid globalization. The latter anthology, which is international in scope, includes only work written during the twentieth century.

Documentary poetry is sustained by concerns similar to those articulated in the poetry of witness, though both its development as a practice and its accompanying critical discourse sometimes differ in significant ways. Particularly in the United States, documentary poetics grew alongside the rise of documentary photography and other documentary forms in the 1930s, in tandem with the organization and mobilization of political reform movements during and after the Great Depression. Documentary activism and poetry aligned in Muriel Rukeyser's collection *U.S. 1* after hundreds of West Virginia workers died of silicosis after digging a tunnel that would divert the New River to generate power for a Union Carbide plant.[25] Rukeyser's principal sequence, "The Book of the Dead," is a poetic assemblage of research on this industrial disaster. As Walter Kalaidjian observed, Rukeyser's poetic treatment of the disaster constitutes

> a modern tour de force in its experimental fusion of poetry with non-literary languages drawn from journalism, Congressional hearings, biography, personal interviews, and other documentary forms. The revolutionary signifying practice mounted in this work effected a key displacement of "literature" itself as a bounded, disciplinary field.[26]

Rukeyser's text sequence rejiggers and even amends the account of the Hawks Nest Tunnel disaster in "an attempt to correct the official record (represented by congressional hearings and coverage in the popular media) and provide the reader with a sense of the connections and complicities omitted from official histories," as Susan Briante puts it.²⁷ In this multifaceted text, we can see detailed research on a well-known historical event play a fundamental and complex role in the poet's craft.

 ## Documentary Poetry

- Begin by having your participants read "Johannesburg Mines" by Langston Hughes, which is available in full above and also online.
- Curate a selection of primary source documents, newspapers, periodicals, and historical sources—the more diverse the better—on a particular historical event or injustice, such as Japanese-Americans' internment in the United States during World War II.
- If you are planning a long session or a multi-session program, have your participants hunt for their own sources in the stacks or via online resources, particularly if your library subscribes to databases that provide access to primary sources.
- From these materials, writers will assemble a range of historical witnesses to the event by whatever note-taking mechanism serves their needs.
- These materials will form the basis of a new poem, in keeping with Rukeyser's assertion that "poetry can extend the document."
- Scheduling time for sharing allows other writers a window into the verses created through this strategy.

Given the social and political consciousness of this sort of poetry, inclusive library collections are particularly crucial. Librarians should recognize Hughes's "Johannesburg Mines" as participating in a long history of African American documentary poetry that arcs toward Black representation and liberation. More recent African-American poets have carried on this tradition; these authors include Natasha Trethewey, whose Pulitzer Prize-winning *Native Guard* (2006) uses historical sources to make poetry out of the history of Black soldiers in the Civil War, and Shane McCrae, whose second collection, *Blood* (2013), draws on archived slave narratives to re-articulate the histories of violence against Black bodies. Claudia Rankine also writes about these subjects in *Citizen: An American Lyric* (2014), partly through documentary sources. African-American

COLLECTIONS OF DOCUMENTARY POETRY

- *Blood Dazzler*, Patricia Smith (2008)
- *Chain, 1994–2005* (journal, edited by Osman and Spahr), https://jacket2.0rg/reissues/chain
- *Coal Mountain Elementary*, Mark Nowak (2009)
- *Dictee*, Theresa Hak Kyung Cha (1982)
- *from unincorporated territory*, Craig Santos Perez (2008)
- *Giscome Road*, C. S. Giscombe (1998)
- *A Handmade Museum*, Brenda Coultas (2003)
- *Jonestown & Other Madness*, Pat Parker (1985)
- *Lake Superior*, Lorine Niedecker (1968)
- *leadbelly*, Tyehimba Jess (2005)
- *Legends from Camp*, Lawson Fusao Inada (1992)
- *Look*, Solmaz Sharif (2016)
- *MACNOLIA*, A. Van Jordan (2004)
- *The Network*, Jena Osman (2010)
- *Ohio Railroads*, C. S. Giscombe (2014)
- *One Big Self*, C. D. Wright (2007)
- *Paterson*, William Carlos Williams (1946)
- *Pierce-Arrow*, Susan Howe (1999)
- *Remember to Wave*, Kaia Sand (2010)
- *Shadow Evidence Intelligence*, Kristin Prevallet (2006)
- *Shut Up, Shut Down*, Mark Nowak (2008)
- *Souls of the Labadie Tract*, Susan Howe (2007)
- Testimony, Charles Reznikoff (1965)
- 12 Million Black Voices, Richard Wright (1941)
- *Voyager*, Srikanth Reddy (2005)
- *Whereas*, Layli Long Soldier (2017)
- *Zero Hour*, Ernesto Cardenal (1980)
- *Zong!* M. NourbeSe Philip (2008)

documentary poetry has ventured into life-writing, as in the bio-graphical verses of Adrian Matejka's *The Big Smoke* (2013), about the first African-American heavyweight boxing champion, Jack Johnson, or Rita Dove's *Sonata Mulattica* (2009), about the biracial violinist George Bridgetower. (For prompts on biographical writing, see our chapter on life-writing.)

While the examples of documentary poetry proceed from histori-cal persons, groups, or events, other poems "containing history" have temporal conceits. With their relationship to occasional poetry—that is, verses composed to celebrate events such as anni-versaries and coronations—these poems reflect a particular time and place. For example, Walt Whitman's poem "1861" attempts to encapsulate the political and social tumult of an entire year, as does John Dryden's earlier "Annus Mirabilis."

 The Annual Poem

- Have your participants read "1861" by Walt Whitman as a model for their projects; this poem is available online at the Walt Whitman Archive: https://whitmanarchive.org/published/LG/1867/poems/ 164
- Ask each participant to choose a different year, or write different years on slips of paper for your participants to draw out of a hat.
- Next, help your participants research their respective years using your library's collections and resources.
- Have your participants write a poem encapsulating that year in the fashion of Whitman's "1861," and share the resulting works.

W. H. Auden's poem "September 1, 1939," commemorates the speak-er's reactions and feelings on the occasion of the outbreak of World War II. Several poets—May Cannan, Isaac Rosenberg, and Vera Brittain, to name three—have written poems titled "August 1914," about the first month of World War I. If your patrons are having trouble conceiving of a historical or documentary subject, they might proceed from a particular date or time period, and perusing something like Chase's *Calendar of Events* may prove useful.[28]

Other Historical Poems

Other poetry activities involving historical sources from your library's collections include the following:

- Have your participants research their genealogies, then select a person from their family tree. Once selected, your participants may research where and when that person lived, their occupations, and other details, in order to write a persona poem from their selected ancestor's perspective.

- Select a town monument and have your participants research the history informing and invoked by that monument. A monument in proximity to the library would be an optimal choice, so that people can view it and its features; alternately, choose one for which you possess ample documentation that allows writers to scrutinize the monument without leaving the library. Their poems based on the monument and their research could be shared with one another or, potentially, at a related civic event.

- Have your participants choose a historical invention or technology, such as the steam engine, the cotton gin, or the telephone. Help them research their chosen technologies and the historical impact these devices have had. Then have them write a poem about that technology, marshaling notes and ideas from their research. For an example, you and your participants may look at Cole Swensen's poem, "The Invention of Streetlights."[29]

- Gather some of the oldest newspapers and periodicals available in your library, perhaps generating prints from microfilm. Use these sources to prompt participants' poems. You could, for example, have them write poems based on particular articles or images, or even around an entire issue.

FOUND POETRY

To some degree, these activities have introduced the possibilities of repurposing found language as raw, malleable material for making and remaking meaning. Found poetry is distinct from documentary poetry in that no language original to the poet is added to the work. This category covers a broad set of practices with different groundings and aims, including complicated relationships to the Dadaist precedent of rejecting meaning altogether. Depending on the creator, different sorts of attention are paid to where a text is coming from and how it has been transformed. Perhaps even more so than the documentary tradition, examples in this form sometimes provoke workshop participants to ask, "How is this even a poem?"

One notable example is Ronald Johnson's 1977 *Radi Os*, which was composed through the process of erasing words from the first four books of Milton's *Paradise Lost* and presenting the remaining text, along with the representative white space, on a nearly vacant page. Two years earlier, Charles Reznikoff published *Holocaust*, a single poem derived entirely from two other books: *The Trials of the Major War Criminals at Nuremburg* and *The Eichmann Trial in Jerusalem.* Reznikoff lineated his source material and reduced twenty-six volumes of documents to a little over one hundred pages in an attempt to more starkly render the testimony of affidavit witnesses. No discussions of law are included, or a single word from the presiding judges. Reznikoff's project and singular achievement exemplify an approach to source material in which a focused body of information must become even more distilled. Reznikoff's work exists firmly within both the documentary and found poetry traditions, though the stress falls more on the former. Johnson's book is an early example of erasure poetry, a form that has proliferated during the last decade and is sometimes called blackout or redaction poetry. The audacity of eliminating language from Milton—or even Shakespeare, as Jen Bervin did with her erasure of the sonnets, published as *Nets* in 2004—is the gambit of effacement that one aspect of the tradition offers. Given that government documents or even inaugural addresses have more recently been repurposed by erasure, we can see a broader pattern emerge here: erasure empowers the reader to talk back to power in its own words, whether that power is embodied in a canonized author or a president.[30] Erasure can also just be a playful challenge, built on the unlikelihood of extracting something beautiful and strange from a remaindered book with the help of a bottle of white-out.

Finally, within the found poetry world, distinct from erasure and quite far from Reznikoff, we might encounter someone like Bern Porter, whose *Found Poems* (1972) combine bits and pieces of communication in more recognizable formats—questionnaires, recipes, and advertisements alongside numbers, graphs, and schematics—alongside material whose source, purpose, or genre remain mysterious. Porter, a polymath who was involved in the development of the cathode ray tube, the Saturn V rocket, and the Manhattan Project, which he renounced after the bombing of Hiroshima, also worked as a publisher, visual artist, and writer. His prodigious output exemplifies a dynamic, promiscuous experimentation within the genre and can serve, in itself, as an easy place to begin.[31]

Examples of poetry that rely on historical texts created by others might open a conversation about what authorship is or means in the age of "remix culture," which Lawrence Lessig calls "Read/ Write culture": a culture in which the consumers of texts also become producers in how they remediate the same texts. In other words, found poetry complicates ideas of what can be thought of as original. Its essential question is this: when does a text become (re)new(ed) through remediation enough that someone else should be acknowledged as its author? Some practitioners of found poetry substantially alter their texts, and some simply transcribe and curate them. There are now whole journals dedicated to publishing found poetry, such as *Unlost* (unlostjournal.com) and *The Found Poetry Review* (foundpoetryreview.com). Regardless of the conclusions one arrives at regarding remix culture, exercises in found poetry can take emerging writers out of their own heads and patterns and also alleviate the pressure of producing more traditionally "original" work. If your participants remain (productively) skeptical, with firmly planted ideas about originality and authorship that make them feel as though using other people's words is cheating, pointless, or dishonest, you can reassure them that it's now standard practice within found poetry to cite the original author(s) when known. Even Walt Whitman, as scholars are now finding out, included found and appropriated text(s) in what American readers may think of as his highly original free-verse lyrics.

Occasions

Upon the death of President Lincoln, Whitman wrote "O Captain! My Captain" and "When Lilacs Last in the Dooryard Bloom'd" as elegies for the beloved national leader. The deaths of public figures and family members have inspired many poems throughout history, such as W. H. Auden's "In Memory of W. B. Yeats" and the late Donald Hall's many poems for his departed wife, Jane Kenyon. Death is just one event that might occasion the writing of a poem. Others include the presidential inaugurations of John F. Kennedy, when Robert Frost famously recited "The Gift Outright" rather than reading a new composition, and of Barack Obama, who asked poets Elizabeth Alexander and Richard Blanco to read original poems following his speeches. The occasions can also be more commonplace. Wallace Stevens's "Sunday Morning" continues a lineage of Sunday morning poems, one he returned to later with "Ploughing on Sunday."

Occasions might allow your writing group to align their practice with the events that are presently shaping their lives. Occasions also allow you to align the objectives of your writing group with other things that might be happening in your library or the larger community, such as holiday displays for Halloween. Happenings your group members might write about include the personal and the political:

- The first day of school
- The birth of a child
- An eclipse

▨ A headline from a current newspaper

▨ A humanitarian crisis

▨ A space travel event

▨ A battle

World-historical occasions might also let you use your library collection, since your writing group could do some research before embarking upon the writing project itself.

SCALE AND PRACTICE

With time, history has changed from a field controlled, at least in Western cultures, by narrators invested in the actions and perspectives of political and military figures to a more open one. Prominent institutions, like Montpelier, are being identified as models of how this type of inclusive history may look.[32] The turn from what is sometimes referred to as "great man" stories to microhistory and social history has added more voices to the field. While librarians do not necessarily need to be drawn into debates about how history should be done, it is worth understanding that most academic historians maintain an allegiance to empirically grounded research, while the infusion of postmodern theory into historical work comes from other, related disciplines. As library users craft their own histories, whether they want to tell their families' stories, or create verse narratives or some more conventionally historical tale, we can guide their access to details that will inform and enrich their stories.

Notes

1. David M. Kennedy, "What Is History Good For?" *New York Times Book Review* (July 16, 2009), https://www.nytimes.com/2009/07/19/books/review/Kennedy-t.html.

2. Joyce Appleby, Lynn Hunt, and Margaret Jacob, *Telling the Truth about History* (W.W. Norton, 2011), 9.

3. Ibid., 59

4. "Sanborn Fire Insurance Maps," Sanborn, https://www.sanborn.com/sanborn-fire-insurance-maps/.

5. "Sanborn Maps," Library of Congress Digital Collections, https://www.loc .gov/collections/sanborn-maps.

6. Kathleen Weessies, "Using Sanborn Fire Insurance Maps Online (Michigan): Links to Sanborn Sites," Michigan State University Libraries Research Guides, http://libguides.lib.msu.edu/c.php?g=96131&p=625797.

7. "Union List of Sanborn Maps," Indiana University Bloomington Libraries Government Information, Maps and Microfilm Services, https://libraries .indiana.edu/union-list-sanborn-maps.

8. Philip Hoehn, "Union List of Sanborn & Other Fire Insurance Maps," University of California at Berkeley Earth Sciences & Maps Library, www .lib.berkeley.edu/EART/sanborn_union_list.

9. "National Union Catalog of Manuscript Collections," Library of Congress, www.loc.gov/coll/nucmc/.

10. "Guide to Diaries Held at the American Philosophical Society," American Philosophical Society, https://search.amphilsoc.org/diaries/search.

11. "UNM CSWR American Indian Oral History Navajo Transcripts," New Mexico Digital Collections, University of New Mexico, http://econtent.unm .edu/cdm/landingpage/collection/navtrans.

12. Jennifer Burek Pierce, Collen Theisen, and Becky Canovan, "Write Your Own Hamilton: Finding Your Story in Libraries," NerdCon: Stories conference (October 15, 2016), https://ir.uiowa.edu/slis_pubs/16/.

13. "Advertising Collections," Duke University Libraries Digital Collections, https://library.duke.edu/digitalcollections/advertising/.

14. "Popular Baby Names," Social Security Administration, https://www.ssa .gov/oact/babynames/.

15. "The Anne S. K. Brown Military Collection," Brown University Library, https://library.brown.edu/collections/askb/.

16. Allen County Public Library Genealogy Center, www.genealogycenter.org/.

17. "Jacob Lawrence: The Migration Series," The Phillips Collections, http:// lawrencemigration.phillipscollection.org.

18. Civil Rights Digital Library, "The Digital Library of Georgia," http://crdl.usg .edu/.

19. Maria Russo, "A Book That Started with Its Pictures," *New York Times* (December 30, 2013), https://www.nytimes.com/2013/12/31/books/ransom -riggs-is-inspired-by-vintage-snapshots.html.

20. Chimamanda Ngozi Adichie, "The Danger of a Single Story," TEDGlobal conference (July 2009), https://www.ted.com/talks/chimamanda_adichie _the_danger_of_a_single_story.

21. Rick Riordan, @camphalfblood, Twitter (July 29, 2018), https://twitter.com/ camphalfblood/status/1023585608302780416.

22. Ezra Pound, *Literary Essays of Ezra Pound* (New York: New Directions, 1954), 86.

23. "Epic," Glossary of Poetic Terms, The Poetry Foundation, https://www.poetryfoundation.org/learn/glossary-terms/epic.

24. Henry Wadsworth Longfellow, "Paul Revere's Ride," poets.org, Academy of American Poets, https://www.poets.org/poetsorg/poem/paul-reveres-ride.

25. "The Hawk's Nest Tunnel Disaster: Summersville, WV," National Park Service, https://www.nps.gov/neri/planyourvisit/the-hawks-nest-tunnel-disaster-summersville-wv.htm.

26. W. B. Kalaidjian, *American Culture between the Wars: Revisionary Modernism & Postmodern Critique* (New York: Columbia University Press, 1993), 162.

27. Susan Briante, "Defacing the Monument: Rukeyser's Innovations in Docupoetics," Jacket2 (April 21, 2014), https://jacket2.org/article/defacing-monument.

28. *Chase's Calendar of Events*, Rowman & Littlefield, https://rowman.com/page/chases.

29. Cole Swensen, "The Invention of Streetlights," The Poetry Foundation, https://www.poetryfoundation.org/poems/54124/the-invention-of-streetlights.

30. Rachel Stone's article in *The New Republic* provides additional background on the form; see Rachel Stone, "The Trump-Era Boom in Erasure Poetry," *The New Republic* (October 23, 2017), https://newrepublic.com/article/145396/trump-era-boom-erasure-poetry.

31. Some of Porter's work is available in free PDF formats at UbuWeb, www.ubu.com/historical/porter/porter_5books.html.

32. Randall Kenan, "The Descendants," *Garden & Gun* (February/March 2018), 99–104.

2

Life-Writing

Life-writing includes biography and memoir, but it is not exhausted by them. It is a broader category that also includes more informal, practical, and fragmentary practices—journals and diaries, letters and testimonies, even shopping lists or "notes to self." Thinking about writing and life means noticing how and where they are, in this age, intertwined. A variety of genres that will interest library users can be collected under the umbrella term that *life-writing* represents. Librarians and writers working at this interface will benefit from a broad concept of genre, as well as an awareness of the different strategies that published writers use to produce their work, and exemplars of the form.[1]

Relationships between comparatively loose modes of documentation that accumulate almost unconsciously during the day and the more established genres of nonfiction are complicated. History, memoir, essay, and investigative journalism offer varying sets of conventions and expectations for published nonfiction, but initial exploratory work does not necessarily have to be informed by any one of them. The focus of this chapter is on supporting and offering input for life-writing, construed broadly, since it would be misleading to think that the only legitimate purpose of life-writing should be the corraling of these more disparate, piecemeal scraps into more recognizable forms like a memoir. Whether the work being made seeks or finds an audience may be secondary to the writer's curiosity and drive to find out what specific things she has to say.

Some diary entries become testimonials to an age, like *The Diary of Anne Frank* or that of Samuel Pepys; others simply remain diary entries. Some shopping lists are only shopping lists, while others might contribute to a study like Michael Hirst's *Michelangelo: The Achievement of Fame.*[2] Outlets for autobiographical narratives are myriad: they appear as self-published family histories that are shared with one's relatives, as Kindle Singles or other digital editions, or they may lead the writer to seek out essay contests in literary journals and other more traditional modes of publication. Life-writing may begin with an inheritance, as with a volume like *The New England Butt'ry Shelf Cookbook* (1969), in which Mary Mason Campbell shared generations of her family's recipes and traditions. The Nigerian writer Yemisi Aribisala extends and complicates this tradition in her recent collection, *Longthroat Memoirs: Soups, Sex and Nigerian Taste Buds* (2016), winner of the John Avery Prize at the Andre Simon Food and Book Awards. The power of life-writing lies in its intimate relationship to the everyday, the given, the things we are already doing. Patrons interested in creating original essays or a memoir may feel like they will be starting from scratch when, in fact, they don't have to. A stray item on an old list of errands might bring back vivid memories from a distant event in one's past. William Gass's "I've Got a Little List," from his collection *Tests of Time* (2003), is the most beautiful essay on this topic, while Shaun Usher's compilation *Lists of Note* (2015) offers 125 examples of the list form that illustrate its capacity for both elegance and surprise.

WAYS OF BEGINNING

Librarians who want to offer guidance to their writing patrons can find an opportunity in our contemporary habits of communication. This section walks you through some ways this kind of work can play out. Beginning with the ways people document their lives, we pay particular attention to how life-writing is already unfolding, and we consider the different degrees of intentionality that accompany its accumulation. We emphasize the roles played by reflection and assessment on the part of writers themselves in shaping and reshaping this material to create a fuller expression of their own voices and stories.

For most digital citizens (and for younger patrons in particular), the practice of life-writing may be closely bound up with particular devices or online platforms, such as text messaging, Facebook updates, and Tweets. This section will consider the particular possibilities created and thwarted by these platforms. The goal is to highlight how we keep track of and share our lives on these platforms and, more specifically, how our contributions on them can be seen as extensions of well-established traditions in life-writing. Despite its general informality, this sort of life-writing can still provide distinct possibilities for a relationship to form, content, and craft, and it is worth considering as a valid literary endeavor with its own freedoms and limitations.

Writing instructors who worry about the negative influence of digital platforms on their students' expectations for prose style often fail to see how these same students are showing a devotion to and desire for communication, much of it written, in their online posts. Libraries that are introducing or developing creative writing skills are in an excellent position to simply draw attention to practices that patrons already engage in online. In this respect, life-writing does not begin from lack but from an overabundance of material. Paired with a recognition of the fact that good writing is often rewriting, this desire for capturing, shaping, and presenting what we are trying to say over the course of our everyday communications can create a basis for beginning to understand craft. Asking what can happen beyond a first draft and noticing the greater depths that become available to a piece of writing as it becomes fuller and more polished through revision are often ready possibilities in the arena of life-writing, precisely because we don't begin by thinking of it as art at all. For some writers, there is a better chance of catching interesting material when it is casually sketched, before we've had the chance to mold and shape it in our own way.

Consider some of the following tactics, keeping in mind that the goal is to create a (temporary) alternative to staring at the blank page; this can begin from one among any number of sources or platforms. The first step is to begin with what a writer has already done, looking through the archive of her writing that is already scattered across physical and digital spaces. This can start with an act of physical gathering to find examples of one's own life-writing, collecting them in an envelope, folder, or binder. As an addition to or substitution for this method, the writer might begin by starting a new document on the computer, then cutting and pasting in a single type of her digital communication from the past week, month, or year, depending on frequency. Writers can decide whether they want to organize their materials according to modes of communication or if they want to try to stitch together, in chronological order, all of the updates, tweets, and text messages they sent during a single stretch of time. If these approaches sound exhausting or simply tedious, make selections: a writer can pick three or four captions from her Instagram feed that are evocative, even without the photo, or find one question sent in a text message that may be interesting on its own terms. Another way to begin is not to worry about your archive at all, but simply to pay attention to your present habits and methods of writing. Again, cut-and-paste is a writer's friend, and there is no immediate need to do any further writing.

We should pause here to consider questions of publishing, privacy, timing, and voice. Facebook functions as a free publishing platform, albeit one shaped by a business model in which users are exposed to advertisements in exchange for the benefits of communicating with large numbers of other online users. There are tensions and trade-offs in this model, just as there are in any other kind of publishing opportunity. Part of the power of such massive platforms is the prospect of immediate sharing, alongside the related prospect of "likes" or retweets from others who affirm that what you just said was insightful, moving, or witty. Of course, being attacked is not the only counterpoint to this; there is also the chance of being ignored or simply less "liked" than you were for your previous post. Most users of social media will recognize this feeling. The more relevant point for our purposes in this chapter is simple: social media barely give you time to have any second thoughts about what you've just written before a lot of other people are telling you what they think of it. Or that they aren't thinking of it at all.

Because there is almost no lag in the publishing process on these platforms, we have to create one. With that in mind, take a break from your online accounts for a week (or just take it one day at a time, if need be), but *keep writing*. It doesn't matter how you do this—typing or longhand, paper or pen—but don't let yourself go silent. You can think of this as saving up material, if need be. The difference is that everything you write is for your eyes only, for as long as you want. This whole experiment begins, obviously, with delayed gratification and the choice *not* to find out in real time how anyone else feels about what you are writing. Instead you have to retain it, keep track of it, and live with it. At some point—maybe on the second day, maybe after a few months—you will probably want to change something in what you've written. Once you have this impulse, which may involve replacing or eliminating a word, reworking a sentence, or expanding on an insight, you are not only crafting a piece of writing, you are doing it on your own schedule and according to your own sense of how it should come off.

There can be at least three tangible opportunities that follow from this activity. One is that it gives writers a chance to reassess their work by encountering it within another setting. A digital document is not the same as a box below the question "What's on your mind?" and a piece of paper is not the same as a screen. These changes in media are significant, simply because they defamiliarize the writing process and give the writer a chance to feel more like the audience, rather than the creator. Secondly, this process will allow writers to discover for themselves how this act of ordering creates narratives, and to see which themes recur, how images cluster and scatter. Even if these things are very discontinuous, the fact that one person has been doing the writing is likely to show up over time. Repetitions that might have been less visible when the entries were treated discretely, once noticed, are something the writer might choose to do something with. Finally, the activity allows writers to assess where the heat is. Where did they write something that was particularly sharp and insightful, more descriptive, or more connected to a complicated feeling? Evaluating your own writing in the space you've given yourself by reapproaching it days later, allows a different kind of internal dialogue to develop than social media encourages. If a writer considers her own social media posts (particularly when they are placed alongside writing that wasn't done on social media), other things can stand out as well. Some of what she encounters might sound precisely like what it is (a Tweet, an Instagram caption, etc.), but other passages might begin to seem like a line of poetry or something that one character could say to another in a scene that hasn't been written yet.

All of this is, of course, a roundabout way of retreating to an earlier, pre-Internet mode of thinking about writing, and to repeat, it is not necessarily superior or wiser—nor is it a cure for anybody's need for external approval. It is simply another way in which writing can be pursued, one which grants the writer privacy to listen more closely to her own voice. This might lead to a different relationship to the practice of life-writing as an end unto itself (keeping a notebook, keeping social media accounts), the abandonment of all social media, or experiments with genres that writers did not necessarily realize they were interested in, above and beyond the Facebook post.

The general strategy here is one of self-enforced *slowing down*—which can be connected to the simple act of trying out different physical modes of writing. Thoughtful deliberation and rapidity of composition may both be tied up with inspiration, but they are also connected to technology; both modes, like every style, will have their own limitations. Writers who can touch-type sometimes prefer to compose first drafts longhand because they have the feeling of typing faster than they can think. Others feel a particular sense of rhythm or embodied weight that is present in the act of using a typewriter. Still others use Dictaphones. Writers need to be reminded that they have options, but they also need to be aware that their habits might be limiting them unnecessarily. Of course, librarians are not responsible for cracking the code that clarifies which medium of composition is actually the most durable, pro-ductive, or liberating one for a patron, who will need to experiment with her own writing process. It is worth reminding writers who are in a creative rut that setting down one set of tools and picking up another can be refreshing.

LIFE-WRITING AND NOTEBOOKS

When a writer tries this shift from posting on social media to keeping a notebook and finds it useful, there is the reasonable follow-up question of what sorts of writing we might put into a notebook. Most of us are likely to feel more confident predicting how things will go in a diary or a journal, which have the built-in advantage of being structured around daily life and the calendar that organizes it. A notebook is more open-ended and less prescriptive about what might belong inside it and what use it might prove to be. Aside from dated entries following the format of a diary entry, how else could a notebook page start?

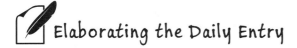 **Elaborating the Daily Entry**

Instead of, or in addition to, saying what you did today in your notebook, you can choose one or more of the following prompts as a starting point for a separate page of writing.

1. List one or more distinct talents that you have and how you became aware of them or fostered them. Minor and/or bizarre talents count.

2. List resolutions you have made (around the New Year or otherwise), and note why you made them and whether you kept them.

3. Try to list all of the friends you've ever had. Put an X beside everyone you've lost contact with. Don't look at Facebook to do this (at least not at first).

4. Choose the ten songs you've loved the most during your life and the people, places, and sensations you relate them to. Try to tell us what is great or simply memorable about each song.

5. List three decisions you have made that you either were or remain deeply ambivalent about.

6. List three decisions you've made that you feel were unequivocally the right ones.

7. List three things you've done in your life that you feel genuinely ashamed of.

8. List five moments you can remember that you would like to relive, for the pleasure that they offered.

9. List five moments you can remember that you would like to relive, because you wish you had done something different.

10. List five meals you will never forget and the reason you won't forget them.

11. List five or more objects that you have lost.

12. List three or more significant lies that you have told.

This sequence could initially be treated as a sort of questionnaire, though that might be a little exhausting. Let's say that you've answered all of these questions to some degree. Now turn back to the list of questions (or your answers) and try to notice where your attention is stuck. A writer doesn't have to know why it is stuck where it is, only to start writing about this particular meal, lie, song, friend, decision, object, or moment in a way that will bring it further into the light. The act of elaborating on the context in which something happened, and developing it into a scene with tangible physical details, demands a significant amount of attention in itself. The idea here is not to stay on topic (in fact, if your item doesn't take you somewhere else, it may not be doing much), but to see where and when you find momentum in these lists and then take that where it leads you.

Here is a partial list of other things that can end up in notebooks: momentary observations, bits of overheard conversation, memories, fragments from the news, frustrations, dreams, open-ended questions, wishes, hypotheses, brief descriptions of people the writer cares about, but also enemies or strangers, long encircling musings on topics that cannot be overcome, jokes, schemes, ridiculous fantasies, promises, strange and strangely specific lists, misheard song lyrics, diatribes, things the writer has forgotten and now relies on others to remember, the names of flowers, trees, animals and galaxies, yoga poses and household gods, books to read and reread, self-reproaches, consolation, speculation, character studies, and famous last words.

In addition to working with prompts or creating other sorts of rules for your notebook entries, it is important to not decide in advance what it is you are trying to describe, understand, or locate with the act of writing. Writing can be a matter of intense, focused concentration, but it can and should also be available to processes of associative thinking: of wandering, improvisation, and discovery that permits you to stumble on things, repeat yourself, change your mind, and lose track of whatever questions you were asking yourself at the outset of your entry. Not knowing what you think until you write it is a strange, recurring experience. But it is also part of what keeps people interested in the process. Trying to immediately determine what scribbling makes sense, is too deeply personal (or impersonal), is sufficiently or insufficiently beautiful, and whether it is original, profound, sentimental, or whatever—all of these are debilitating to the process. Every writer knows this and struggles all the same, but it is one reason to have a particularly loose and informal notebook that allows the writer to find out what she wants to say by writing. A notebook can be a space of periodic discovery, intermixed with lots of redundancies, half-formed thoughts, and dead-ends. It is the excess of the notebook that makes it useful. Adding to it is more like turning over compost than sprucing up a garden.

Writers may find it useful to establish specific points in the day when they have time to sit for a long period with a notebook, but it is more important to consistently keep the notebook nearby, since thoughts may occur only briefly and at strange times of day. Also, with any luck, you will find yourself wanting to make use of the notebook that you keep at hand at all times simply because it's there. You'll start to notice yourself seeing more, pushing harder to get thoughts into strings of words, and becoming more comfortable depositing verbal energy onto the page. Writing this way is not about getting better, really, but about gaining a different awareness of yourself and your surroundings. The second self you have on the page—your written self—is something that will begin to emerge and feel more recognizable to you as you add to it and continue to pay attention to your own voice. It may be annoying or embarrassing to discover that you have certain tendencies and ticks in your writing, particular words and phrases that you return to through habit. But this doesn't make you a terrible writer. It simply means that you are an individual writer. Developing a critical eye and ear for these facets of your own style means that you will be in a better position to distinguish between the moments when you are being your best, written self and when you are simply falling back on a mode that comes easily to you.

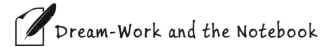 ## Dream-Work and the Notebook

Writers seeking to set up a simple rule for notebooking or trying to get out of a rut may want to try devoting part or all of their journal to the transcription of dreams. Dreams are inherently interesting to the dreamer, and this form of creativity occupies a fascinating, indeterminate place between genres (are they fiction or nonfiction?) and is unique because it happens on its own terms. Putting a notebook or Dictaphone at your bedside and catching your memory of the dream before it evaporates can be challenging, but it is much easier than the deliberate, painstaking construction we usually find ourselves in the midst of while writing.

Dreams can often be found interspersed in the notebooks of writers and are occasionally published as independent collections, as with Vladimir Nabokov's *Insomniac Dreams* (2017), William Burroughs's *My Education* (1995), and Federico Fellini's *The Book of Dreams* (2008). A potentially more interesting alternative to simply compiling dreams is explored by Lydia Davis in her collection *Can't and Won't* (2014). Scattered throughout this book are short fragments of prose subtitled "dream pieces," which she offers an explanation for at the book's conclusion: "Certain pieces I am calling 'dreams' were composed from actual night dreams and dreamlike waking experiences of my own; and the dreams, waking experiences, and letters of family and friends."[3] Alongside an earlier gathering of some of these pieces in *Proust, Blanchot and a Woman in Red* (2007), Davis cites the precedent of Michel Leiris's *Nights as Days, Days as Night* (2017), a book of less than 200 pages composed over 30 years. Looking at either Davis's or Leiris's book, the broader strategies involve taking moments out of waking life that contain something uncanny and strange, then placing these beside actual dreams to sustain a newly wavering sense of the real. The benefit of this practice is that it encourages a different kind of alertness to the everyday, an ongoing act of attending in order to see what is happening in front of us, or just past our sight.

TO WHOM IT MAY CONCERN

While keeping a notebook begins with the assumption of privacy, letter-writing is predicated on the hoped-for attention of an audience beyond the writer, whether it is one specific person or a larger and more general audience. While the decline of letter-writing in contemporary culture has been frequently observed and sometimes lamented, there hasn't been a disappearance of epistolary forms in literature, such as epistolary novels composed entirely of letters to and from various characters in the book. This longevity speaks to the durability of the epistolary form, even when it is only a fictional device, and this gives us another reason to pay more attention to it. Letters in a work of fiction can focus and triangulate specific acts of narration, creating occasions for informality and productive uncertainty. They can also heighten a reader's sense of eavesdropping, and they can chart the shifting distance between people. Like diary or notebook entries, they also lend themselves to seriality and often become part of larger, recurring structures.

If we include e-mails as letters, it is possible to retrace the steps outlined in the previous section in order to consider the life-writing we've already been doing. While such an exercise obviously favors those who never clean out their in-boxes, the de facto archive that piles up from sending and receiving e-mails can be worth sifting through, both for sentences that are interesting in themselves and as a spur to further writing.

Sometimes a letter is simply a way of beginning: "Dear Mr. President" or "Esteemed Members of the Committee" might lead to something you simply wouldn't have said otherwise. Addressing a loved one, an enemy, or a deceased relative creates a sphere of permission in which the writer can imagine what she might say, if such a communication were possible. The unsent letter, or the one to which no reply is possible, pushes the act of writing from the circuit of everyday communication into the tradition of poetic apostrophe.

Reading through letters or e-mails from the past may be disorienting or embarrassing as often as it is pleasantly nostalgic. If we are going through old correspondence not as sentimentalists but as writers on the hunt for some small part of the past that has been captured vividly, in clear and memorable language, we are also likely to be struck by how much searching we have to do. Lots of what goes into letters and e-mails is chatty, hurried, and trivial. We might wish that this previous version of ourselves had taken an extra moment to drop in some extra detail or allowed a thought to wander slightly. The oblivion of forgetting that surrounds a letter might not feel so complete once you start combing through your letters from the past. The poet and essayist Mary Ruefle makes this point more forcefully:

> Every time you write an unengaged letter, you are wasting another opportunity to be a writer. The greater the disparity between the voice of your poems [or stories, or essays] and the voice of your letters, the greater the circumference of the point you have missed. The demands upon you, as a writer, are far greater than you could have guessed when you filled out your application form and mailed it. How far are you willing to travel this love you profess to have for words?[4]

COMMONPLACING

Another strategy for gathering material is the keeping of a commonplace book, wherein a writer copies out evocative or useful passages from the work of others. This is another old method with contemporary and digital analogues but, as with the previous two examples, the work has more to do with reframing existing pieces of writing than with reinventing the wheel. The historian Robert Darnton describes commonplacing as

> a special way of taking in the printed word. Unlike modern readers, who follow the flow of a narrative from beginning to end, early modern Englishmen read in fits and starts and jumped from book to book. They broke texts into fragments and assembled them into new patterns . . . Reading and writing were therefore inseparable activities . . . you could read your way through [the world]; and by keeping an account of your readings, you made a book of your own, one stamped with your personality.[5]

It's this very last action of stamping a book of commonplaces with an individual personality that gives the practice its value. It points to a different concept of creativity and authority than we may be accustomed to, one that is in many ways closer to a curator than to traditional conceptions of the creative writer. We should remind ourselves, though, that we are thinking about the broader compositional category of editorial decisions, and commonplacing allows the writer to develop a private stockpile of language that feels, or once felt, useful and provocative. This set of decisions could extend to the question of whether or not spoken language and dialogue will also be incorporated into one's commonplace book or not, for example.

Keeping a commonplace book is a way of experimenting with unoriginality. As an extension of life-writing, we can understand it as a particular practice in which, by copying another person's words, you are suspending the distinction between reading and writing. Rather than a microphone or a camera, you are the recording medium. What gets copied, whether it is a line of poetry or a paragraph of prose, depends on the judgment of the writer. In fact, one way of thinking about the practice of commonplacing is that the unit of composition is not the story, essay, or sentence but the *decision* about whether to include a particular passage. Pithy quotations have always, understandably, been preferred to extended arguments, but there are no hard-and-fast rules as to what can and cannot go into a commonplace book. Unlike the foregoing examples we've touched on in this chapter, copying and pasting is antithetical to a true commonplace book, whether handwritten or typed. The usefulness of commonplacing for the copyist is that the physical act of copying the relevant passage teaches you something about how it unfolds as a thought and how it was constructed as a piece of language. The commonplacer isn't aspiring to become a photocopier or to duplicate a reference work like *Bartlett's Familiar Quotations* but to learn something through osmosis.

While something resembling this practice can be traced back to at least the medieval era, commonplacing really found a foothold during the Enlightenment, when it was inseparable from the education of many famous writers and intellectuals. Present-day discussions around appropriation, copyright, and intellectual property are actually secondary to the more basic assumption of the commonplace book: when a writer takes the time to re-create a passage she admires, she is able to attend to it in a way that is distinctly different from simply passing her eyes across the page. It isn't necessary to take this idea on faith. Brief or sustained experiments with commonplacing should inform each writer whether there is anything in it for her. Even if it proves to be a useful practice, the keeper of a commonplace book has certain decisions to make when undertaking a separate piece of writing: Do I try to rework this language into an articulation of my own? Should I try to quote directly, then outrun the shadow cast by that author's insight or observation? Or should I keep the quote like a secret, letting my new writing speak back to the quote without placing the latter directly onto the page where my rejoinder to it will unfold?

 Stitching a Frame

There are innumerable ways to arrange and conceptualize the fragments that a writer copies down from others. Instead of trying to exhaustively cover them here, we will acknowledge only three. The first is the most conventional: the fragment as an epigraph or an inserted quote, either at the beginning or in the midst of the text. A constraint that may or may not be necessary is to require writers to limit themselves to one quote. This might make it easier to talk about how one's text grew out of, or formed itself as a response to, that particular passage. Librarians should have no challenge finding poetry and prose to use as examples.

The second form is a segmented, serial approach to quotation. It requires the writer to construct a work consisting of multiple sections, each of which will have its own title, which should be drawn verbatim from a particular text by another writer. These titles can be entire sentences or mere phrases, taken from one source or from several, as in the case of Jenny Boully's essay "There Is Scarcely More Than There Is," which appears in *[one love affair]** (2006) and cites Gertrude Stein, Samuel Beckett, Djuna Barnes, and Robert Walser across its fifteen sections. Another example of such an approach, this time using a single source, is April Freely's 2015 essay "Stand Your Ground," which takes each of its headings from James Baldwin's 1953 essay "Stranger in the Village" and can be accessed online.[6]

As you share one of these works with your group, encourage participants to consider what kinds of dimensionality become available within this constraint. How would they describe the resulting forms of the text? How does the sustained company of another writer, or a small circle of them, create a different sort of conversation within the work? What authors will your participants invite into their own texts?

The final strategy for using a commonplace book is to allow it to remain what it is and simply continue adding to it. E. M. Forster's *Commonplace Book* (1987) or W. H. Auden's *A Certain World* (1970) offer two examples from canonized British authors. Giacomo Leopardi's *Zibaldone* (1898) is a monumental, maximalist work, weighing in at over 2,500 pages and providing an example of an engagement with the form that is also one of the writer's most important works.

LIFE-WRITING AND DISPLACEMENT

Writing in diaries and notebooks can work quite readily on a daily basis, but it is a mistake to think that your clearest insights into the present will happen on that same day. Ernest Hemingway is often cited for his speculation that "maybe away from Paris I could write about Paris, as in Paris I could write about Michigan. I did not know it was too early for that because I did not know Paris well enough."[7] This is one reason why life-writing, as a process that begins in practices like keeping a notebook, diary, or commonplace book, can take a little while to accumulate possibilities. An alternative is to start drawing from the life-writing of others.

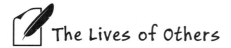 The Lives of Others

Have the writer choose a particular entry, note, or letter in a collection of writings from an author that she feels somewhat familiar with or curious about. Collections of diary entries or letters by other writers lend themselves to selective reading, so it is relatively easy to zero in on a particular point in time (a war breaks out, the subject finds her record at the top of the charts, she meets or begins a correspondence with another figure of interest, etc.) and begin from there. One criterion could simply be whether or not the writer feels interested enough to reread the passage of text. After doing so, she should simply set the book aside and try to use what she encountered as the basis for a few pages of new writing. This can take any form she wants, including a list of questions. Another option would be to use some of the details in the entry and begin trying to flesh out an entire scene from them.

Alternatively, the writer can try to place the writing of this entry into the day that the author actually lived—for example, what did Darwin do after he finished up this note and set it aside? How did its preoccupations cling to him for the rest of the day and the one that followed? You can consider changing the point of view and playing with scale. For example, choose a single detail in an entry that is more profound and resonant if it stands alone, or let your own writing continue exploring the world that this document offered a window into for as long as possible. For inspiration, you can turn to richly imagined and extensively researched historical novels like Hilary Mantel's *Wolf Hall* (2009), Michael Cunningham's *The Hours* (1998), and Marguerite Yourcenar's *Memoirs of Hadrian* (1951). The past always starts speaking from somewhere.

A NOTE ON MEMOIR

One of the goals of this chapter has been to emphasize that life-writing and memoir are not synonymous, though the latter remains the place where blockbuster moments are most likely to happen within the wider field. Library resources can offer a way for memoirists to check their memories against the actual record of public events, trace parts of their own genealogy, or delve further into the details of the times and places that framed their lives while remaining mostly opaque to them, perhaps because they were children or simply uninterested, or perhaps because they were traumatized. This last aspect of memoir-writing is easily the most complicated one to consider and, for library staff, it is a place where they should be particularly cautious. While poems, stories, or essays can all include subject matter that is fraught territory for the writer by being deeply connected to painful life events, a memoir carries a different set of expectations and risks in this area by making no pretense to being a pure fabrication (James Frey's *A Million Little Pieces* created a scandal precisely because it breaks this contract with the reader). The authorial self shaped on the pages of an autobiography is a character, and the writer's memory can be selective and unreliable. This does not dissolve the difficulties inherent in responding to written work that testifies to a terrible moment in the writer's past and, in the context of such disclosures, it is impossible to think only of what the narrator is doing or saying, and not about the person in the room.

The limits of what writing and reading can do mean that our commitment to this kind of creative writing program will need to be guided by some ground rules. You should outline your expectations and ask for input as you clarify how trust and respect can be maintained within the group you're working with. At the very least, you should talk about trigger warnings. Additionally, you may want to acknowledge that while writing can be a useful part of therapy, it is not the same thing as therapy. One obvious but crucial difference is that a therapist is paid to listen to you and help try to make sense of what you're getting at, while an audience will not be. Writers should be aware that it is possible, in writing about trauma, to actually achieve a sort of breakthrough on the page, articulating a truth they had not realized it was within their power to articulate. This is one of the most powerful things that can happen for any writer. It is also possible to re-traumatize yourself by making the work public, through print or sharing it at a reading. There are no quick guides on this issue. Library professionals should remember that caution is not necessarily the opposite of creativity and that it is not up to them to tell a writer when and how to best protect herself from such experiences, any more than they can tell her what to write about in the first place. While there is a large body of thought about the many dimensions of trauma and writing, as this book goes to print, discussions in connection with the #MeToo movement are particularly pressing.[8]

Finally, resources for writers working along these lines include Mary Karr, whose book *The Art of Memoir* (2015) should be in your collection, along with Vivian Gornick's *The Situation and the Story* (2001), because these are the two best books on the genre. "In some ways," Karr writes, "writing a memoir is knocking yourself out with your own fist, if it's done right."[9] This is another way of saying that memoir-writing is not for everyone, that it doesn't have to be, and that even though it has attracted skeptics, it has also developed its own mythos. Perhaps memoirists have been unfairly labeled as an intensely inward-looking set, but in all fairness, this is how most writers are usually viewed. Because there is only so much a librarian can do to facilitate artistic introspection, it's worth considering how Rebecca McClanahan speaks about the interweaving of an author's own story, insofar as it relates to both a family and to the wider historical landscape:

> If recording a particular family's history is the sole motivation a
> writer has, then the audience for the writing will probably be quite

small. But when that history collides with something larger than the facts themselves—whatever that something is—the chances for connecting with your reader grow. That something might be language, or it might be characterization, structure, voice, theme, research, or I-search, anything that helps the writer escape the given, those facts that already exist outside of the writer's experience with them. Yes, accuracy matters; facts matter. But how do they matter? That is the key question for me.[10]

If part of what defines the writer's work is this willingness to take on the task of examining both the tools of the craft and this shifting, variegated range of factual *stuff* that could also be called material, the librarian is someone in a strong position to tell them where more of the mess is. Together, these sustained acts of attention are one way of continuing to ask how both writing and life keep company with one another and continue to age, contest, and stay curious about how they might mean together.

Notes

1. As a supplement to the present chapter, both librarians and patrons may find it useful to explore the extensive online resources of the Oxford Centre for Life-Writing at https://www.wolfson.ox.ac.uk/oclw.

2. Michael Hirst, *Michelangelo: The Achievements of Fame* (New Haven, CT: Yale University Press, 2012).

3. Lydia Davis, *Can't and Won't* (New York: Farrar, Straus and Giroux, 2014), 289.

4. Mary Ruefle, *Madness, Rack, and Honey* (Wave Books, 2012), 211–12.

5. Robert Darnton, "Extraordinary Commonplaces," *New York Review of Books* 47, no. 2000) 20): 82–87.

6. April Freely, "Stand Your Ground," New Madrid Journal (February 2015), https://newmadridjournal.files.wordpress.com/2015/02/stand-your-ground.pdf.

7. Ernest Hemingway, *A Moveable Feast* (New York: Scribner, 1964), 7.

8. See Julia Jacobs, "Using Young Adult Novels to Make Sense of #MeToo," *New York Times* (September 12, 2018), https://www.nytimes.com/2018/09/12/books/me-too-young-adult-fiction.html; Ricci Yuhico, "The #MeToo Movement: Teens Research the Fight for Women's Rights," Stuff for the Teen Age, New York Public Library (May 23, 2018), https://www.nypl.org/blog/2018/05/23/metoo-teens-research-womens-rights; and Leigh Anne

Jasheway, "The #MeToo Movement and Its Impact on Women's Writing," *There Are No Rules,* Writer's Digest (March 29, 2018), www.writersdigest .com/editor-blogs/there-are-no-rules/industry-news-trends/metoo-movement -and-its-effect-on-womens-writing.

9. Mary Karr, *The Art of Memoir* (New York: HarperCollins, 2015).

10. Sharon DeBartolo Carmack, "An Interview with Rebecca McClanahan," *The Writer's Chronicle* 47, no. 5 (2015): 79–90.

3

Making and Manners

"There are things / We live among 'and to see them / Is to know ourselves,'" George Oppen tells us at the beginning of his long poem "On Being Numerous."[1] The promise within things and the possibility of perceiving what is integral to us depends, in part, on asking who made something, how it was produced, and for what reason. These questions drive any number of investigations, real and fictional. Starting from this perspective, if what a culture makes is central to what it is, we can consider manners and other cultural cues as made things as well. These social cues, in turn, reflect the possibilities and limitations of their milieu. More broadly, our sense of words appropriate to our social roles or the apparel we choose for an occasion are manufactured or tailored for particular needs and purposes that exist within a wider era. We are what we make, but we are also how we treat one another. These intertwined aspects of invention and tradition orient the present chapter.

Making and manners are strong currents in daily life, working in tandem to define social roles and situations. Despite lingering traces, their origins may now be obscured. The "self-made man," for example, was a person whose wealth and reputation depended on his own efforts rather than on inheritance. Part of the way readers recognized these characters, the way they signaled what contemporaries saw as their only recently respectable status, was through their clothing; their manners or behavior, however, nonetheless revealed their humble origins. Terry Pratchett's *Dodger* (2012), which places the Artful Dodger from *Oliver Twist* in a central role, both relies on and plays with this type of transformation. As Dodger gains influence and a little more money, he changes his wardrobe. It is a shift mirroring the way the original character's role in Dickens's book is revealed by his hat and his use of a "man's coat," so large that it "reached nearly to his heels." In both novels, the character's speech and ethics remain constant. Dodger's apparel, and that of every other person until well into the twentieth century, was more often made by hand than by machine. If, as the saying goes, "Clothing makes the man," for centuries clothing was, if you will, man-made. This chapter brings the themes of clothing and manners together to look at how writers might research and create strong, authentic language that shows aspects of making and manners. By focusing on depictions of apparel and etiquette, authors can engage facets of writing that are traditionally said to make up a story, such as character and setting, or work toward larger, more abstract themes.

Another way of talking about making involves the language of craft. While an inclination to distinguish between art and craft endures in some fields, we are drawn toward the philosophy Ann Shayne attributes to the Bauhaus School, which operated in Germany between 1919 and 1933: "Bauhaus pioneered a synthesis of art, craft, and design that broke down previous distinctions between 'fine art' and 'craft' (read: stuff you look at versus stuff you use)."[2] The British Arts and Crafts movement of the late nineteenth and early twentieth centuries also espoused the idea that, given the effort of making and the place of things in one's daily life, beauty and utility should be aligned. (Our decision to write about art separately, in chapter 5, reflects the long-standing genre of ekphrasis, or literary writing about visual art.)

Authors have used the tensions between the signals sent by a character's clothes and his conduct to tell stories. The things people wear or aspire to wear often prove integral, revealing a character's identity in ways that prove pivotal to plot, as in Maupassant's story "The Diamond Necklace." Similarly, the thought of the things we lack but still desire sticks with us and creates motivations. Other classic stories, like Cinderella's dilemma in dressing for the ball and Tom and the Prince's exchange of the former's "rags" for the latter's "splendors" in Mark Twain's *The Prince and the Pauper,* allow characters to experience new social environments, expanding their horizons and perspectives. We see these dynamics again in Andy Sachs's efforts to fit in at a fashion magazine in *The Devil Wears Prada* (2003). In Sarah Prineas's *Ash and Bramble* (2015), the nameless narrator contrasts her own rough apparel with the delicate stitches she is expected to produce, and she understands her role in the story through these contrasts. All of these are examples of what Linda Grant, in *The Thoughtful Dresser* (2009), describes as "clothes as text, clothes as narration, clothes as a story. Clothes as the story of our lives."

Elsewhere, manners maven Judith Martin has interpreted the "language of clothing" as "high symbolism." We can see this dictum at work in John Singer Sargent's portraits. Deborah Davis's book *Strapless* (2003) focuses on Sargent's once-controversial 1884 painting now known as *Madame X,* with its obvious correction of the sitter's fallen shoulder strap. That garment, as Sargent depicted it, was judged by contemporaries to be too suggestive. In part because of this earlier stigma, the painting still garners commentary. This image of a confident woman wearing what we might regard as the Victorian version of the little black dress, considerably *avant le lettre,* defied social conventions by suggesting a sort of independence and sexuality then seen as inappropriate. Her clothing expressed disdain for convention, resulting in both furor and fascination.

Another, quieter Sargent portrait depicts *Elsie Palmer,* daughter of the man credited with founding Colorado Springs. The Palmer portrait is known by two names, that of the sitter and a more abstract title that emphasizes its iconic aspects, *Young Lady in White.* Like the painting of the striking French socialite, Elsie Palmer alone features in this nearly life-sized painting. Unlike the earlier image's depiction of a sophisticated woman in a close-fitting black dress, with her face in profile, Palmer wears white and stares directly at the viewer. The contrasting apparel and attitude, however, form another commonality: their mutual divergence from conventions of dress. The portrait of the young woman shows her in ankle-length skirts appropriate for an adult of the era, but her hair is not dressed; instead of a chignon or ringlets, her straight, dark blond hair is cut with blunt bangs and falls below her shoulders. These portraits use clothing to say something about their subjects, and the ensuing century of critical reaction to the apparel and attitudes they portray tell us about the society both of their time and of today. These paintings are only two examples of the ways that writers might draw on representations of clothing (and the commentaries upon it) as part of their research on apparel for particular times and places.

Articles and Odes

Linda Grant has argued, "If you were to gather all the clothes you have ever owned in all your life, each baby shoe and winter coat and wedding dress, you would have your autobiography."[3] In this exercise, you should direct writers to select one item of clothing that they are either wearing or that they recall from a moment of their personal history. The aim is to describe that item and its valences, what it is and what it says about the wearer, the time in which it was worn, and so on.

Alternatively, or if time permits, you can have participants give this article of clothing to a fictional character who should appear in a scene of at least one page or so. For poets, consider sharing Pablo Neruda's "Ode to My Socks" as a model of both seriousness and play.

As these examples suggest, clothing and art can play off each other, as ways to think about surface and structure. Clothes are things that we both try to write about and that we encounter as made objects and media images, whether found in current magazines or archives. They are tangible things that can be held or turned over in the hand, and they are also things that are represented to us as flat or moving images that lack their original dimensions. How do aspects of their form and presentation create a framework for both description and the possibility of putting other ideas, characters, scenes, and images into contact with them? Writers can think of the way people can inhabit or be inhabited by their clothing—and experience the world differently because they're navigating it within an outfit.

TO LEARN MORE ABOUT CLOTHING IN RECENT YEARS

▨ Tim Gunn, with Ada Calhoun, *Tim Gunn's Fashion Bible: The Fascinating History of Everything in Your Closet* (New York: Gallery Books, 2012). This book explains the everyday clothing worn by Americans in the present and how it came to be, comparing the wardrobe to "the range of words in your vocabulary" (1). It starts with the premise that clothing is a function of time and place: "The shapes you like best and the fabrics at your disposal are connected to the era in which you live" (52). This general guidance, along with Gunn's informed engagement with a range of specifics, offer the researcher a great set of starting points for considering the role of apparel in a story. The book also discusses the clothing styles of earlier eras. Gunn notes, for example, that it wasn't until the twentieth century that it became normal for women to wear skirts and separate tops, rather than dresses (100–101). He links the present association of pink with girls and blue with boys to post-World War II sensibilities (166). Time shapes norms, and ideas about what is appropriate, sufficiently formal, decent, or respectable are continually renegotiated. T-shirts were originally sold as undergarments, and their emergence as costumes for rebellious characters in mid-twentieth-century movies reflected their questionable status as street wear (27). Gunn's book makes it easy to see how clothing could both define a character and prompt conflict with others whose ideas about appropriate apparel are different.

▨ Charlotte Mankey Calasibetta, Phyllis G. Tortora, and Bina Abling, *The Fairchild Dictionary of Fashion* (2002). Now in its third edition, this is the definitive volume on how stylistic features of clothing are labeled and described. Thousands and thousands of terms, accompanied by illustrations, fill its 500 pages. Writers looking for ways to accurately describe fashion will find no more authoritative resource than this book. Although it is somewhat pricey, older editions are available from many online booksellers.

■ *Contemporary Muslim Fashions* is a museum exhibition, an online presence (including a Facebook group), and a book by Jill D'Alessandro, Reina Lewis, and Laura L. Camerlengo. Fashion designers' creations and individuals' striking Instagram images are profiled and curated through the London-based de Young Museum's activities. Writers seeking to understand Muslim fashion as something more than the fleeting images on news channels will benefit from the voices and perspectives reflected in the media collected here (https://deyoung.famsf.org/exhibitions/contemporary-muslim-fashions).

■ Museum at the Fashion Institute of Technology (http://fashionmuseum.fitnyc.edu/). Although this museum focuses on actual garments, highlighting notable design, its website allows users to search the collection virtually, with broad, initial categories reflecting different time periods. Thumbnail images represent each searchable item, and each image can be expanded and is accompanied by a description of the maker, the materials, and the period, creating insights into the nature of couture apparel and trends. Users can create an account to save images of clothing and accessories, past or present.

■ Valerie Steele, *A Queer History of Fashion: From the Closet to the Catwalk* (Yale University Press, 2013). This edited collection focuses on the role that fashion has played in the LGBTQ community from the early eighteenth century to the present day. Accompanying an exhibition of the same name, this lavishly illustrated collection ranges across the lives and work of designers and style icons, examines the relationship between fashion and social activism, and argues for the centrality of queer culture in the creation of the modern fashion industry. The book won the Milla Davenport Publication Award in 2014.

▨ Graham Marsh and JP Gaul, *The Ivy Look: An Illustrated Pocket Guide to Classic American Clothing* (London: Frances Lincoln, 2010). Despite its name, *The Ivy Look* offers insights into far more than prep apparel. It is, effectively, a photodocumentary of modern American style. Filled with reproductions of 1950s and 1960s menswear ads, exemplar celebrity photos like the *GQ* cover that proclaimed Miles Davis the best-dressed man of 1961, and album covers, this little book is a treasure trove of American style and the surrounding culture. As aficionados of a particular genre of vintage apparel, Marsh and Gaul ensure that the book's photos provide details, whether of "original 1950s Army-issue khakis" (116–17) or the features of an alligator-bearing Lacoste polo shirt (143). Stores and manufacturers are also discussed, serving the needs of writers who might want to send their characters shopping.

▨ *The Sartorialist* is both a blog and a book of urban street fashion. This popular and ongoing blog was developed by the fashion photographer Scott Schuman in 2009, and selected images from it were eventually released in book form. Though mostly taken in New York City, his photographs also depict apparel from other major cities around the world. His work might be seen as a glossy extension of the tradition of the fashion photographer Bill Cunningham (1929–2016).

▨ Trinny Woodall and Susannah Constantine, *What Not to Wear* (Weidenfeld & Nicholson, 2002). *What Not to Wear* became a minor infotainment empire, with the original BBC television series spawning multiple books and eventually an American remake. Books by the series' original hosts could prove useful to writers who want ways to signal either a character's flattering look or a frumpy one. The TLC series also saw spin-off books by host Stacy London, notably *The Truth about Style* (2012), so whether library users are interested in the British original or the iterations popular in this country, both books and videos support explorations of how clothing and body type work together . . . or not.

Famous men are often remembered for their style, even if we typically pay more attention to what women wear. Presidents are more likely to gain notice for their sartorial choices when they mix things up in some way. Either famously or infamously, John F. Kennedy is said to have sent the hat industry into a fatal decline by his refusal to wear one while serving as president. Commentators who considered Barack Obama's tan suit to be a threat to national security were not unlike those scandalized by the glen plaid suit Ronald Reagan debuted on a European trip.[4] Interestingly, it seems as though a potentially cartoonish accessory, like Franklin Roosevelt's cigarette holder or Donald Trump's too-long, tape-fastened red ties, can be incorporated into the image of a president by means of consistent repetition. In contrast, presidential wives have tended to find their daily decisions about what to wear in public a renewable opportunity for either accolades or ridicule. Each First Lady's apparel is now commemorated by an exhibition of significant dresses at the Smithsonian Institution (http://americanhistory.si.edu/first-ladies/first-ladies-fashions). Spanning the period from Martha Washington's painted silk dresses to the present, the display attracts long lines of determined viewers, particularly when a new inaugural ball gown is added. Together, these dresses reflect traditions, changing conventions, and personal style.

One modern First Lady noted for her style allows us to examine both the way clothing is represented and how it can be researched. Numerous narratives and resources focus attention on Jacqueline Kennedy Onassis, a member of the Bouvier and Auchincloss families, the wife and widow of a president, and a fashion icon even in her years as an editor at Viking Press. In picture books, in fiction, in nonfiction, and in movies, the clothing that Jackie Kennedy wore is central to how she is seen on screen and on the page. Interestingly, one author who writes about her wardrobe and style calls attention to the way media served as metaphors for her outfits. To one contemporary writer, she appeared much as "a woman out of a Cole Porter lyric," while another described her as "looking like a fashion magazine illustration."[5]

Jackie Kennedy's clothes, and the glamorous and sometimes surprising choices she made, form a plot point in Ann Hood's *The*

Obituary Writer (2010). Hood's characters obsess over the First Lady's wardrobe, and there is no shortage of sources that allow a writer to look back over those outfits. *Jackie: The Clothes of Camelot* (2002) includes newspaper photos, designers' sketches, and some details about the decisions involved in the First Lady's public appearances and private choices. Images from the Kennedys' May 1961 state visit to Paris revealed a couture wardrobe created by Givenchy; the anticipatory conversation that Hood's characters indulge in as they await Kennedy Onassis's appearance is grounded in the fact that many details about her wardrobe for this trip and other occasions "had to be kept a secret."[6]

Another beautifully photographed and richly detailed book, *Jacqueline Kennedy: The White House Years — Selections from the John F. Kennedy Library and Museum* (2001), contains new and contemporary images and research. This book, with essays by Kennedy experts, provides pictures that allow us to see the structure of an item of clothing, as well as the way it fit and looked *in situ*. Given that Jackie Kennedy wore outfits to multiple events and sometimes traded clothing with her sister, the book's notes about where and when the public first saw a dress offer insights into the much-reproduced Kennedy style. The red wool suit featured in ads for the film *Jackie* (2016) appears in these pages, and readers will observe that the movie's costumer faithfully reproduced the suit's color, texture, and shape.[7] In interviews, the costumer observed that the plentiful photographs of the Kennedys and the enduring public interest in Jackie's look were factors driving the demand for verisimilitude in the movie.

 Functional Style

Writing focused on Jackie Kennedy has sometimes sought to explain the power of her image by analyzing what her choices of clothing connected to, functionally or symbolically. Wayne Koestenbaum notes that many "quintessential Jackie outfits implied athleticism; maybe she required simple clothes so that she could run away from crowds and cameras. Think of Capri pants (slacks had their own minor radicalism, if only because Jackie Kennedy's predilection for them outraged a Republican dowager): Capri pants urge us to get lost. Think of sandals for Mediterranean shopping; pants for walking around Manhattan; sweater tied around her neck, as she hails a cab after work."[8]

    With this passage as an example, you can prompt writers to use an accessory or article of clothing as a vehicle for speculation and description. You should encourage participants to notice how Koestenbaum moves away from the figure of Jackie Kennedy to personal associations with Capri pants and sandals, before returning to her at the end of the sentence. Whether worn by themselves, someone else, or a fictional character, how does a cloak, a hoodie, a kerchief, or a necklace of cowrie shells evoke a particular set of expectations and connections that tell us something about the person who put them on?

With 2018 news articles on the rediscovery of notes planning her wardrobe for the fatefully interrupted 1963 trip to Dallas, what Jackie Kennedy wore signals not simply style but occasion.[9] These kinds of choices connect clothes to the province of etiquette. They are choices that have changed significantly over time, and the formality of dress that was the norm not so many years ago may now strike younger users as unusual. We have used Phillip Hoose's *Claudette Colvin: Twice Toward Justice* (2009), with its photographs of the Montgomery bus boycott, in our classes. To those who lived through those years, the civil rights protesters' clothing is unremarkable; to generations accustomed to a more casual dress code, the dresses and suits that the protesters wore reveal something other than normal respectability. These differences mean that we must encourage writers to look at how clothes would have appeared when contemporary, rather than simply what they say to us. We don't need to ignore or set aside our immediate reactions—distinctive descriptive language might arise from them—but we do need to contextualize them, looking at whether what is perfectly ordinary to us might, in fact, have seemed outrageous or unusual in its time, or vice versa.

WRITTEN AND UNWRITTEN CODES

Since their origins, etiquette books have dictated appropriate apparel, and many more recent titles in this line continue the tradition. From the typewritten, mimeographed "Coed Cues" that once cautioned young women at the University of Dubuque against coming "to dinner looking like the end of a three-day bike race" to the 1995 republication of *The Amy Vanderbilt Complete Book of Etiquette* with its five pages of commentary on appropriate workplace dress, sources telling us what to wear at different times and in different places abound.[10] Sometimes, however, it wasn't simply convention that dictated what could be worn. In Elizabethan England, laws regulated apparel according to rank.[11] Known as sumptuary laws, these codes defined what was appropriate to a person's social standing. Excessive spending and costly, attention-getting dress could be punished with jail time. As the Folger Library explains, "Since clothing defined people by rank and income—or in effect 'made the man'—the laws' primary targets were those who attempted to make themselves something other than what they were."[12] Sumptuary laws were overturned by the next monarch, but dress codes, if only in the guise of popular fashion, endured. Regulating dress has long been a means of regulating society and the people who constitute it, creating multiple dimensions for writers to consider as they outfit their characters.

Sometimes what etiquette books do is explain social situations to people who are new to them and who lack access to any other reliable authorities. These volumes proliferated during the Industrial Revolution, when people left farms and small towns for jobs in urban areas made possible by mechanization and modern industry. Etiquette manuals articulated desired behaviors for people who found themselves in new roles and away from parents or other guardians who might explain and enforce conventions. These guides governed both personal conduct and the emerging norms of changing professional life, such as typewritten business correspondence. Writers interested in learning how a letter would have read in a previous era, and what it would mean to observe an epistolary convention or to deviate from it, might find it expeditious to consult these guides, rather than surveying myriad period letters. One relatively recent etiquette guide won an award from the Reference and User Services Association in 1963. *Service Etiquette* was recognized for its comprehensiveness, and that is what makes it valuable to a writer who wants to understand U.S. society in the decades after World War II.[13] Although its primary audience was military men and women, *Service Etiquette* tells a writer much about how life has changed since the 1950s. Where we have cell phones at our disposal, making phone calls a reflexive and unthinking act, long-distance phone calls were costly when this book was written. *Service Etiquette* explains how to send a telegram to reserve a hotel room at one's destination (197). It cautions against writing indelicate letters, advises readers on how to eat novel foods ranging from avocados to tortillas, and describes the conditions for performing an arch of swords for a bride and groom as they depart their wedding in a military chapel (362). The book also advises servicemen on what to wear when not in uniform. A book of this sort, then, is a writer's best friend when it comes to the details of life in days before one's own.

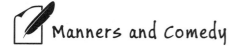 **Manners and Comedy**

As an exercise, select a rule or norm from an etiquette guide, like the use of silverware at a formal dinner. Writers of fiction could create a scene in which one of their characters confronts this convention for the first time. Writers of nonfiction could explore the way that this norm has changed in the years since the guide's publication. The smallest shifts, missteps, and distinctions can incite or complicate a variety of narratives. The novel of manners, as exemplified by Jane Austen, Edith Wharton, and Henry James, is built upon observations of difference in comportment and demeanor as indicators of social class, with the goal of rendering the social fabric of a single time and place. Writers might discover that when they try to figure out or explain why a social convention is being followed, their explanations often lead to more questions, parallel rules, and more stories. If writers struggle to pinpoint an interesting social convention, encourage them to write about a moment when they witnessed or perpetuated a breach of social conduct. What was the fallout? Did they know better? Do they think it's a stupid rule? Would they do it again? Why or why not?

Alternately, writers can try an experiment with literary estrangement. Horace Mitchell Miner's classic satire "Body Ritual among the Nacirema" (1956) is frequently taught in social science courses, since it deploys anthropological language about ritual, daily routine, and a cultural hero called Nontgihsaw ("Washington" spelled backwards) to describe the cultural practices and beliefs of Americans (i.e., the "Nacirema" spelled backwards).[14] By inverting names and hewing to the curious, distanced style that anthropologists traditionally use when writing about cultures outside their own, Miner's satire also provides a striking example of what Russian formalist critics termed "defamiliarization" or estrangement, which they considered a central literary value. You can challenge writers to select a particular routine, nicety, or cultural commonplace that they can make peculiar on the page not through grotesque exaggeration, but by attending to details and shifting their style just enough to make the moment mysterious. The goal is not to be vague, but to find new, unorthodox ways of presenting something so normal it has become invisible. In many ways, the participants will be making a piece of writing that works with the intrigue and playfulness of a riddle. At the conclusion of the exercise they should share their attempts with their peers to see how they did.

Certainly, writers relying on etiquette manuals for a sense of another era or culture need to consider that sometimes rules are reiterated because they are being challenged. Lest it seem that these treatises are musty, fussy bastions of regressive norms, we would point to *Miss Manners' Guide to Excruciatingly Correct Behavior* (1979). In this humorous and informative book, Judith Martin provides witty explanations of eighteen-button gloves (arm-length women's gloves measured, per French convention, by the diameter of a button, 546) and the demise of cocktail dresses because "it has become quite unfashionable to lead a life in which you are at liberty to go home and change your clothes at five in the afternoon" (547). To an inquirer who asked, "What am I supposed to say when I am introduced to a homosexual 'couple'?" Martin famously replied, "'How do you do?' 'How do you do?'" (67). Regardless of the era in which they are written, etiquette books reflect their authors' personal convictions as well as the prevailing social conventions. Writers might be advised to check for any particular author's bias or liberality by consulting multiple guides from the same era.

MAKING LIVES, ILLUSTRATED

- Anna Mason et al., *May Morris: Arts & Crafts Designer* (London: Victoria and Albert Museum/Thames and Hudson, 2017)

- Jenny Uglow, *Nature's Engraver: A Life of Thomas Bewick* (New York: Farrar, Straus and Giroux, 2006)

- Kate Davies, *Handywoman* (Edinburgh: Makadu, 2018). There is a related TEDx Talk at https://www.youtube.com/watch?v=HPla wa_pIMY.

- Emma Bridgewater, *Toast and Marmalade: Stories from the Kitchen Dresser*, A Memoir (London: Salt Yard Books, 2014)

- National Museum of the American Indian, Smithsonian Institution, "Native Knowledge" (https://americanindian.si.edu/nk360), and the NMAI Blog (http://blog.nmai.si.edu/)

In considering fashion guides of earlier eras, another well-documented aspect of making is the work involved in creating clothing and other objects by hand. The do-it-yourself and maker movements have been through a number of revivals since the nineteenth century, when skilled craftsmen responded to mass production with antipathy.[15] To itemize all aspects of making would be impractical, so we offer here a few illustrative examples to suggest possible avenues for research and inquiry.

First, there are the increasingly popular handcrafts of knitting and related fiber craft. Debbie Macomber and Gil McNeil are among the popular contemporary novelists who incorporate knitting into their storylines, recognizing the need for patterns to shape one's work and instruction in order to become proficient. Writers will find further examples of connections between text and textiles in independent publishing, such as Larissa Brown's publications of knitting patterns, like the one for her Lichen shawl, and her historical novel, *Beautiful Wreck* (2014). It is important to recognize that machine knitting did not replace hand knitting as a means of making clothing until many years after its introduction; initially, machine knitting was technically possible, but it was limited in capability and expensive. In other words, writers should not assume that knitting or crocheting is a synonym for "old-fashioned." If a writer seeks to understand knitting in its historical context, two broad treatments are Richard Rutt's *History of Hand Knitting*, covering Great Britain, and Melanie Falick's *Knitting in America*. Numerous blogs and YouTube videos demonstrate knitting techniques (authoritative sources include Mason Dixon Knitting and Purl Soho); this matters because some of those same blogs discuss well-known representations of knitting that are incorrect, to the point that the way the needles are represented would render them useless to an actual knitter.[16] If a writer's aim is authenticity, then an awareness of what knitting tools would be appropriate, the conditions of their use, and other details can keep a narrative from becoming clunky or hitting false notes.[17]

Fiber work extends beyond knitting into less domestic arenas. Some of the same materials, terms, and techniques play out in the making of sails, to offer a single example, and sails figure in everything from vintage children's books like *Swallows and Amazons* to Patrick O'Brian's beloved *Master and Commander* series. Some writers describe splicing, a technique for joining two separate fibers or wires without knotting them, as a "lost art" integral to "repairing the rigging on a sailboat."[18] Sailing is likewise concerned with the canvas fabric of sails, and one company that began making that material 130 years ago as a family business still has an employee who recalls its operations before "we got our first phone or when the diesel engine came along." A key detail, beyond testimonials to the way sailmaking was done before newer technologies facilitated it, is that there is also continuity in these older modes of production. Then and now, the canvas for sails and commercial projects "moves across the same machines, using the same sewers."[19] The manner in which sails and other canvas-based objects are made, as well as their material and technique, is distinctive here, and a writer invested in waterfronts as a setting could benefit from learning about the workings of people who make life on the water possible. If a writer envisions, say, a sail tearing at a critical moment, leaving her characters with a problem to surmount in order to resume their journey, what conditions would have wrought this sort of devastation? What means did unfortunate sailors have to repair equipment damaged or destroyed by the elements?

A further small but tantalizing element of sailing in times when so much was done by hand expands our sense of the knowledge necessary to these undertakings. As Dean King and John Hattendorf explain in *Harbors and High Seas* (1996), "The captain of a large sailing ship needed skills and experience in two broad areas, requiring quite different types of knowledge." Knowledge of a ship included "how to operate and repair her rigging and sails, how to care for the health and morale of her men, and how to maintain and use her charts, logs, navigational instruments, and guns," but also "how to be a ship handler and voyager who knew how to make the best use of the winds and ocean currents all over the world."[20] Those documents and instruments were created by hand and by handmade tools, and a knowledge of the maritime environment, King and Hattendorf tell us, "took half a lifetime to master."[21] It is not writing technique alone that informs plot or action; King's remarks make clear that the time involved in gaining and synthesizing the necessary knowledge factors into the pacing of a story or novel, and perhaps the characters' temperaments, too.

When writers want to learn about some less common practice, we need to help them find experts. One resource that enables us to do this is Associations Unlimited, a database derived from a print resource formerly known as the *Encyclopedia of Associations.* Using the subject index or keywords in a tool like this is one means of helping writers find makers, regardless of their craft or era. For example, other components of boats besides their sails are still handmade, at least selectively. There are recognized experts in building wooden dories, the old boats that were once essential to New England commerce. Associations Unlimited guides us to the groups with recognized expertise in this area, which in turn will guide us to the Wooden Boat School and *The Dory Book,* which continue to educate people about the making of eighteenth- and nineteenth-century coastal boats. Sailmaking and wooden boats may seem like esoteric examples of inquiry, but we suggest that they serve as hints of the full range of what it is possible to make; they are reminders that in a world of iPhones and high-speed Internet service, people retain and continue to practice older forms of knowledge and technology.

CONCLUSION
Making and Playing

This chapter has outlined some sources of factual information for writers' research into manners and making, but it is crucial to remember that making is often playful. D. W. Winnicott defines play as "relaxed undirected mental inconsequence." This sort of deeply engaged, meaningful play connects the past to the present and absorbs "our concentrated, deliberate attention, deliberate but without too much of the deliberateness of trying."[22] Shaping a pot on the potter's wheel, weaving a rug, carving a sculpture, as well as articulating a line of thought or pursuing a piece of research: all of these, at their best, fall into this sweet spot that Winnicott is describing. They ask for sustained effort without becoming sites of excessive anxiety, strain, or stress. The work undertaken is being done for its own sake and will be evaluated as much for the pleasure it provides as for the perfection of the crafted object. These are values that have a great deal to do with creative endeavors of any kind. Moreover, in addition to considering how purposeful information-gathering can flesh out the social or historical settings that writers want to invoke or the fictional characters they want to build, it's worth emphasizing how discovery also arises from unstructured, less intentional activities. Thus, if the library serves as a site of both investigation and play, librarians supporting creative writers will need to consider how these activities depend on each other, and give library users license to simply continue poking around, almost aimlessly, to see what holds their interest, rather than culling their collections for what pertains directly to a literary undertaking, whether a story, poem, play, or essay.

Notes

1. George Oppen, "On Being Numerous," in *New Collected Poems* (New Directions, 2008), 163.
2. Ann Weaver, "How to Color: A Cheerful Guide for Knitters," Mason-Dixon Knitting (July 26, 2018), https://www.masondixonknitting.com/color -cheerful-guide-knitters/.
3. Linda Grant, *The Thoughtful Dresser* (New York: Scribner, 2009), 79.
4. Elena Hilton, "Four Years Later, I Can't Stop Thinking about Obama's Tan Suit Controversy," *Esquire* (August 29, 2018), https://www.esquire.com/style/ a22862882/obama-tan-suit-anniversary/.
5. Jay Mulvaney, *Jackie: The Clothes of Camelot* (Macmillan, 2001), 31, 63.
6. Ibid., 141
7. Hamish Bowles, ed., *Jacqueline Kennedy: The White House Years: Selections from the John F. Kennedy Library and Museum* (New York: Bulfinch, 2001), 70–71. (This book was published in conjunction with the exhibition held at the Metropolitan Museum of Art in New York, May 1–July 29, 2001.)
8. Wayne Koestenbaum, *Jackie Under My Skin: Interpreting an Icon* (Macmillan, 2009), 118.
9. Bonnie Wertheim, "Jackie Kennedy's Packing List for Texas, Chic and Poignant," *New York Times* (July 3, 2018), https://www.nytimes.com/2018/ 07/03/fashion/jackie-kennedy-texas-packing-list.html.
10. Nancy Tuckerman and Nancy Dunnan, "Behind the Eight Ball," in *The Amy Vanderbilt Complete Book of Etiquette Entirely Rewritten and Updated* (New York: Doubleday, 1995).
11. See "Elizabethan Dress Codes," British Library, www.bl.uk/learning/ timeline/item126628.html.
12. Karen Lyon, "The Rise and Fall of Sumptuary Laws: Rules for Dressing in Shakespeare's England," Shakespeare & Beyond, Folger Shakespeare Library (September 8, 2017), https://shakespeareandbeyond.folger.edu/2017/09/08/ sumptuary-laws-rules-dressing-shakespeare-england/.
13. Brooks J. Harral et al., *Service Etiquette*, 2nd ed. (Annapolis, MD: U.S. Naval Institute, 1963).
14. Horace Miner, "Body Ritual among the Nacirema," Wikisource, https:// en.wikisource.org/wiki/Body_Ritual_among_the_Nacirema.

15. Rebekah Willett, "Making, Makers, and Makerspaces: A Discourse Analysis of Professional Journal Articles and Blog Posts about Makerspaces in Public Libraries," *Library Quarterly* 86, no. 3 (July 2016): 313–29.

16. See Elizabeth Bird, "Famous Illustrators' Depictions of Knitting Ranked in Order of Competency," *School Library Journal* (September 23, 2016), http://blogs.slj.com/afuse8production/2016/09/23/famous-illustrators-depictions-of-knitting-ranked-in-order-of-competency/.

17. Gertrude Whiting, *Old-Time Tools & Toys of Needlework* (New York: Dover, 1928, reprint).

18. Ryan Willms, "Wm. J. Mills & Co.: Crafted with Pride in USA," *Inventory: A Curation of Ideas in Product, Craft, and Culture* 1, no. 2 (spring-summer 2010): 139.

19. Ibid., 132, 135.

20. Dean King and John B. Hattendorf, *Harbors and High Seas: An Atlas and Geographical Guide to the Complete Aubrey-Maturin Novels of Patrick O'Brian* (New York: Henry Holt, 1996), 10.

21. Ibid.

22. D. W. Winnicott, *Playing and Reality* (New York: Routledge, 2012), 147.

4

Amplifying Images

Writing and visual art have had a lot to say about each other for almost as long as both have existed. Paintings have functioned as illustrations of Greek and Roman myths and legends, biblical episodes, and noteworthy historical events since ancient times. Conversely, there is a long tradition of ekphrasis; that is, literary works which describe or comment upon visual works of art. This long, intertwined tradition shouldn't intimidate our patrons, though. Feeling curious about or inspired by art is all that is required for them to join other writers whose creativity is sparked by objects of art. The literary tradition of ekphrasis approaches the archive by way of looking at pictures rather than by sustained reading. It also allows aesthetic questions of focus, balance, beauty, verisimilitude, and vividness to be an immediate, demonstrable part of a writer's engagement with her subject. Some works of art history may be very well-written but their goal is not to provide a literary experience. In contrast, the creative writer seeks to turn an art object into a way of generating new poetry or prose.

Writing that seeks to be artful by attending to an already existing work of art does so with a useful and durable tension. To put it bluntly: why would anyone write (or read) an extended description of a work of art, rather than simply looking at the actual work or a reproduction of it? Why would we need a writer to tell us what's in a Frida Kahlo self-portrait, since the portrait already exists? These are not new concerns, and in fact they contribute to the dynamic within many, if not most, ekphrastic texts.

A piece of great ekphrastic writing depends upon the author's ability to take a singular experience—her encounter with an art object—and make the particular way that her own nervous system and associative mind react to this work into a riveting reading experience unto itself. The text can and should send the reader back to the art object, but ideally, this should be because the reader has been given new eyes with which to view it. Ekphrasis activates this relay between the work of art, the text about the work, and the reader's attention.

For example, poems like William Carlos Williams's "Landscape with the Fall of Icarus" and W. H. Auden's "Musee des Beaux Arts" offer something more than an explanation or summation of the content within Pieter Bruegel's *Landscape with the Fall of Icarus*—they are demonstrating a way of seeing.[1] Each poet is interested in the way that Icarus's fall into the sea has become a miniscule and almost unnoticeable detail within Bruegel's otherwise conventional landscape painting, but the reader's perception of the painting changes shape, at least in part, because of the differences in diction and line length in the two poems. Though Auden and Williams have distinct formal approaches, each is fundamentally following Bruegel's meditative lead in their reflections upon the painting.

More recent and radical approaches can be found in Tisa Bryant's *Unexplained Presence* (2007) and Robin Coste Lewis's National Book Award winner *Voyage of the Sable Venus* (2015). Both books seek out representations of blackness within European works of art, such as the Thomas Stothard etching that Lewis reclaims for the title sequence within her collection, one she describes as "compelling, if you can wipe from your mind that it's a pro-slavery image."[2] Both of these books move across a range of media to reframe the black figures that have been rendered peripheral, ornamental, or debased in artworks manifesting a distinct, racist legacy of sense-making. Bryant and Lewis pursue a different sort of sense by way of contestation, reading the visual rhetoric of their source material against the grain and illustrating one way for ekphrasis to move beyond extended praise. In her preface, Bryant discusses the demands that such an undertaking makes on the attention of the writer:

> As with lovers and spies and secret codes, we're conditioned not to look too long or too closely at how or why these figures do what they do, how they might perpetuate or debunk myths around race, sexuality, storytelling. We simply minimize, as needed, their effect on the environment (narrative), and on us, by shielding them . . . from our view.[3]

Speaking back to art that provokes us and keeps our attention implies a willingness to take on the challenges inherent in writing something that is just as compelling as the picture. Sometimes this work of art might be fictional or mythic, rather than actual, such as the hundred-plus lines rendering Achilles's shield in book 18 of Homer's *Iliad*, or the painting at the center of Balzac's short story "The Unknown Masterpiece." The writing will stand or fall based on its ability to show what a particular painting did to the writer—not simply to transfer its subject material to another medium, but to convey something about the interaction between the two sensibilities. The reader is eavesdropping on that conversation, one in which Achilles's shield or Frida Kahlo's self-portrait is reinterpreted by the attention, needs, and chutzpah of the writer. The alternative to full-on fabrication, then, is competition.

Ekphrastic texts insist on their own point of view, their own ambivalence or wonderment when confronted by a work of art. Many of these texts hover somewhere between an homage and a tug-of-war. When introducing activities that depend on writers choosing their own artwork to respond to, librarians will probably notice that writers' first impulse is to write about a work they think is perfect and love unequivocally. This doesn't necessarily lead to the most interesting or responsive pieces of writing. Trying to be adequate to a work that is widely considered a masterpiece, or simply one that we deeply admire, can actually stack the deck against feeling empowered to loosen up and really express something beyond "Wow!" Finding artworks that have been overlooked, by contrast, can create an entirely new sense of intimacy with the artist and an urgent need to say why *that* faint outline of a child's mouth in Cezanne's sketchbook has something small and perfect about it.

These considerations guide our advice to librarians who want to help writers feel inspired by art. Prompts for this kind of writing, ideas about partnerships with other art-invested organizations, and selected resources that can support art-based writing and programming follow. The nature of art and artistic media might make for more variations or more possibilities than some other subject matter. This chapter, then, is about the many possibilities for writing about art, rather than about a single way to get this programming right.

Variability and Genre: Framing Writing Activities

Consider three ways of beginning a free-writing activity:

- For the first prompt, you ask participants to select some episode or moment from their past, based on a particular variety of memory (one with scary weather in it, or cousins, or a substitute teacher, etc.).

- For the second, you turn the lights down and project an image captured by the American photographer Helen Levitt, known for her street scenes, against a screen, asking participants to write whatever comes to mind.[4]

- For the third, you bring everyone to the nearest window and ask them to observe and write about what they see outside as they see fit.

None of these is a bad prompt, but it's worth pausing to consider why, for some writers, responding to Levitt's photographs will be easier than looking out the window. A work of art is an intentional object, seeking to create and manipulate particular patterns and intensities within our perception. A great work of art shows us how to see and how to keep looking. It can provide a sounding-board that is not a blank page or a mirror, but rather a place to work out language and ideas that might not otherwise be available. Levitt's photographs may lead a writer down an entirely different path than the one originating in her image, one in which the writer says something more intriguing or startling about his own life, or whether he is sparked by a memory or vague intuition about what happened just before the shutter opened.

There is tremendous variability in the responses that art provokes from any given writer. Abstract paintings may fail to say anything at all to some writers, while for others they may create a different kind of space for language. Some writers may not feel compelled by paintings as a general rule, while finding music, film, or fashion an immediate stimulus. Often it helps for the writer to feel that she already has a certain amount of traction with a work, form, or artist, rooted in some previous knowledge, in order to produce an aesthetic response that is pertinent, resonant, or cagey. At the same time, no one necessarily knows in advance what will point them in a useful direction. While dismissing entire art forms from consideration isn't necessarily helpful when starting an ekphrastic practice, these limitations may, temporarily, help writers find someplace to begin.

Sharing resources and suggestions with patrons is a trial-and-error process that depends on the willingness of both the librarian and the writer to keep a dialogue open, share enthusiasms, and respond candidly, without letting their differences in taste override a curiosity about the broader exchange.

LIMITATIONS TO DESCRIPTION

Extended description is not all that ekphrasis is, but it is a start. The risk, if the writer decides that she will also end there, is that a sustained description of a fixed object will end in stasis. This might be desirable, particularly in short literary forms, but as a piece of writing grows, the question of how to create and sustain momentum comes with it. All of these are choices that a writer has to make for herself, of course, but when she senses that the act of description has run its course or simply wants a change in approach, here are some possibilities.

The first is to simply turn the page. Consider other works by this particular artist, or other examples within a genre, time period, or style. This often means dipping a toe into the scholarship around one or more of these categories, which can feel intimidating, depending on the patron's background and how specialized the secondary material is. It might also seem to be beside the point of ekphrasis, which places a premium on the writer's direct impressions rather than on digesting critical work, but this is usually a false opposition.

Writers who worry that knowing more about what they are observing is going to contort or pollute the authenticity of their experience are entitled to this opinion, but if they are serious, it's difficult to see how useful a library can ever be for their practice in the first place. Librarians might remind hesitant participants that the goal hasn't actually changed: they are not suddenly being asked to add to the scholarship on a work. They are simply following their curiosity in an unsystematic way, looking for new questions and little radiant details. A writer may be fixated on the way a distinctively warm yellow tone works in a particular Renaissance painting and feel she has described it to death. Will her writing change if she finds out that painters from the era often used a mineral called orpiment to achieve such a color, that this material was also used by alchemists, and that it yielded sulfur? The process of culling and shaping this sort of information can be just as important for a poem, essay, or story as the act of observation.

Many artists are reluctant to speak about their own work, usually insisting that it should speak for itself, and sometimes maintaining a studied, deflective stance in interviews. Occasionally, though, an artist will offer up language that is much more striking than biographical summaries of the work usually manage. For example, most capsule biographies of Wassily Kandinsky will mention that he experienced synesthesia, associating musical notes with individual colors, but it is a different thing to read Kandinsky describing this experience: "At times it seemed to me that whenever the paintbrush . . . tore away part of that living being which is a color, it gave birth to a musical sound."[5] It is not simply the process of replacing a clinical term with a first-person rendering in which sound and color are animated by Kandinsky's own elegant language—readers are now getting a little bit closer to the distinct, intense sensibility that he brought to his work. For a writer grappling with how to represent this particular multisensory experience, it might make particular sense to listen to Kandinsky's own words, letting them interpenetrate the writer's act of looking.

The best reason for a writer to turn to secondary resources is also the most straightforward one: she has questions that the work itself can't answer. How long did it take to create this piece? Is it a stand-alone piece or part of a series? Is it the work of a famous artist or of his studio and apprentices? Who has owned it, and where has it traveled? As information professionals, librarians are well-positioned to help writers pursue these kinds of inquiries, some of which gird a work like Edmund de Waal's *The Hare with Amber Eyes* (2010).

Avoiding the dilution of what compelled the writer's response in the first place is important, but it is a broader challenge for the process and craft of the practitioner. Each writer will have to use her own judgment to determine when her project is continuing to develop and when it is overbuilt. Avoiding the latter may mean choosing a mode that swerves between the descriptive and the distracted, between being critical and getting swept away. A writer's divided feelings are almost always more interesting than her certainties. Ekphrasis is simply more open, contortion-friendly, and potentially confused than scholarship or journalism. It doesn't fundamentally know what it will do, which is what makes it interesting.

Ways of Writing about Art: Thirteen Prompts

In addition to these general encouragements, here are some prompts that will give writers options for exploring other avenues within ekphrastic writing, beyond writing as vividly as they can about what they see.

1. *Consider your methods of composition.* Don't try to write anything at all while attending to the artwork. Then find someplace where you can no longer see it and write as long as you can to see what happens, or take notes and impose other kinds of strictures on yourself: write nothing but verbs for ten minutes, then ten minutes of only nouns. Give

yourself two minutes for adjectives and let the notebook sit overnight. Then come back to it the next morning and try composing a poem, story, or essay that will use each word you've collected. Let this sit for another day and then write another text in which you cannot use any of these words.

2. *Wander off topic.* Allow yourself to write about what is keeping you from attending fully to the artwork you're trying to pay attention to. Give free rein to your ability to free-associate.

3. *Change your point of view.* The first-person perspective of a viewer engaging the artwork is one option, but it is not the only one. Writing from the point of view of the artist or of a figure depicted in an artwork might offer other possibilities. The sitter for a portrait, whether he is anonymous or a royal, has a view, an outlook on the world. So does a sleeping cat. Ventriloquizing the point of view of whoever we are scrutinizing through the artist's eyes and allowing that voice to talk back can be a way of creating a different tone inside the work, one that can mix with or replace the one that has already been established on first glance.

4. *With a more abstract work, is it possible to craft a voice that fits itself to the feeling the work emits?* If crafting a voice for Louise Bourgeois's spider poses one kind of challenge, something else is required to imagine the murmur within one of Agnes Martin's hand-rendered grids, which she first began creating after thinking about "the innocence of trees."[6]

5. *Seek out a work depicting a crowd.* Photographs can provide one starting point, but so can a large painting like Gustave Courbet's *The Burial at Ornans.* What is the relationship between the central figure and the peripheral ones within a work? How much do the people in the crowd have to say to one another? What are they thinking about instead of speaking?

6. *Imagine another viewer encountering the work you're writing about.* This may be as straightforward as speculating about the impression being made on the stranger standing behind you in a museum. You can also imagine someone you will never meet staring into the same image at the same time. What led that person to pause at the sight of that work? Repeat this exercise, moving as far in time or space as you want.

7. *If imagining the experiences of others isn't working for you, seek out a place where art is on display and pay attention to the patrons there.* Eavesdrop. Do your best to simply seem studious, rather than revealing yourself as a spy. Once you can no longer wander nearby, find a corner of the museum and write for twenty minutes, doing your best to imagine what their lives are like.

8. *Write a description of the afternoon in which the artwork was created or started.* Consider making it one of the less consequential things that happens over the course of that day. Notice the people adjacent to the artist. What are they in the midst of?

9. *Find out enough about the material history of a work to imagine how its journey could have been otherwise.* Imagine when it could have been destroyed in a fire, sold for scrap, or abandoned in despair. If you are tired of writing about works on paper or canvas, look into the history of silent films, as has been done by Brian Selznick in *The Invention of Hugo Cabret* (2007).

10. *Find a work whose creator is anonymous.* In the absence of leads, create a life on the page for that unknown artist.

11. *In a similar vein, try to find out enough about an artist to know his influences or peers.* Now fabricate another artist whose influence was just as crucial but whose work has either been unacknowledged, forgotten, or suppressed. If you are looking to thicken the plot, consider how stolen, forged, or misattributed works might also provide a motor for your narrative.

12. *Mimic the formal approach that an artwork takes.* You can use collage, distortion, chance, smudging, incising, burnishing, pulverizing, repetition, deep focus, and so on.

13. *Borrow or stream a movie you have never seen and turn the sound off.* Write the dialogue as it seems to be unfolding. If you are prone to reading lips, choose something in a language that you don't understand and turn the subtitles off. Alternatively, turn on public radio and turn the sound so low that you can barely hear anything. Then listen closely and try to transcribe what the speakers are saying.

TWO-WAY STREETS

One alternative to seeking out someone else's visual art is to consult or make some of your own. While this has the distinct advantage of sidestepping the problem of access, it obviously runs the risk of falling into excessive self-involvement, a mindset that ekphrasis can actually be helpful for stepping away from. That being said, writers who either already have some sort of practice as visual artists or are open to developing one might be interested in seeing how it could work in tandem with whatever writing they are doing. Librarians do not need to take on the additional task of becoming art instructors. Instead, they might make patrons more aware of relevant resources that already exist. This might mean highlighting the presence of community art classes or, as will be elaborated in this section, pointing out some of the examples of people who combine the visual and the verbal in their work.

One area in which patrons are unlikely to need much prompting is photography. Since the widespread use of smartphones has made almost all of us into amateur photo-documentarians, some writers may find that their own digital archive provides another kind of starting point for a variety of projects. Librarians might emphasize, if they are working on a more formal prompt incorporating patrons' own photos, that writers don't have to decide in advance what they're up to when assessing their shots. It also isn't necessary to know whether or not a piece of writing will need to be presented in addition to the image it's responding to, or whether it will stand in for it completely. Photos might just create the scaffolding for a project so that, once the pages are written, the images that prompted them can simply be removed.

It is worth remembering that even if the cliché about a picture being worth a thousand words is half-true, incorporating visual images onto the page can also run the risk of making the writing superfluous. The ability of the reader/viewer to see and discern something from an image has to be respected, so that the writing will not repeat what has already been presented visually and become redundant. Teju Cole, an internationally distinguished novelist, essayist, and photographer, described the formal challenge of combining the two more extensively than he had previously in his book *Blind Spot* (2017). At different points in the work, he explains that

> what I'm writing about is different from what I photographed. Sometimes they coincide. I don't want my photography to be an illustration of the text. I want the photograph to hold its own. What is the light doing? How are the colors working? How do things balance? The narrative also has to meet the demands of storytelling, of obliqueness, of compression. It has to detonate in a certain way that might actually be adjacent to the photograph, not sitting right on top of it. Which is why I don't really call these texts "captions." They are voice-overs. They are running parallel. Each has to emanate its own energy.[7]

Admittedly, these are exacting standards, but they are also a reminder that captioning a photograph is not the only way language can interact with it. Other relationships are possible. Some writers may find that it is their own relationship to the photographed image and how it punctures, bends, or contains time that creates a space in which they can begin to explore their own sense of the past. Sally Mann, who gained fame and notoriety for her photography before winning the Pulitzer Prize for her memoir *Hold Still* (2015), has a fascinating ambivalence about the art form she is most associated with:

> Before the invention of photography, significant moments in the flow of our lives would be like rocks placed in a stream: impediments that demonstrated but didn't diminish the volume of the flow and around which accrued the debris of memory, rich in sight, smell, taste, and sound. No snapshot can do what the attractive mnemonic impediment can: when we outsource that work to the camera, our ability to remember is diminished and what memories we have are impoverished. (301)

For our purposes here, the point is not to settle upon the ultimate merits or faults of photography as a medium, but simply to notice that it often gets people talking and saying interesting things. Making use of photos also entails a recognition of their limitations, that they are supplemental to the act of memory, of creating a fuller sense of time, place, and sensation on the page where they may (or may not) appear.

MEDIA, MUSEUMS, AND REPRODUCIBILITY

Libraries are, of course, far from the only places where people can encounter art. There are, however, several distinctive roles libraries can fill that are related to their core missions. A local library can serve as an information hub that reveals how and where collections, exhibitions, and public installations of art can be accessed throughout the community. In addition to highlighting work that might be in the library itself, librarians might consider compiling a list or map of places, whether museums, parks, businesses, or public buildings, where patrons can engage art firsthand. Partnered programs with these institutions are also a possibility. Another option being explored in different permutations in Minneapolis, Denver, and Iowa City is lending art itself, allowing patrons to check out individual works for set periods of time.[8] In any case, the opportunity for librarians to use ekphrastic writing as a framework for getting patrons into more direct contact with art will manifest in different ways within any community. The reality, for communities where opportunities to view visual art firsthand are scarce, is that reproductions will be more relevant. And here again, libraries can have a distinct and crucial role.

Let's reconsider our previous example of the Helen Levitt photo, which we have downloaded as a digital file, now standing three feet tall on a projector screen at the front of a darkened room. This image can be used as a writing prompt, but also as a demonstration and as an incitement to a different but related investigation into the image. Let's say that the image is famous enough and the librarian has been willing to trawl the Internet long enough to find three or four different versions of it, each of which is shared in quick succession. In one, the black-and-white image seems overlaid with a yellow or brownish haze. In another, the resolution is noticeably finer and more detailed. And perhaps another image has been cropped drastically or given a distracting caption. None of this is likely to shock writers, who are probably as familiar with the perils of Google image searches as the librarian is. Pointing out how this problem poses a distinct challenge for writers who want to respond to visual art takes an additional resource, namely, a high-quality reproduction of the same image in an art book. Passing around a version of the image as reproduced in a book published by Phaidon, Rizzoli, Taschen or, in Levitt's case, powerHouse Books, creates the opportunity for a different kind of discussion. Aside from its materiality, the quality of the image, its difference in scale, and the context within which the writer is viewing it are all much more likely to enrich the experience of the work's particularity. It isn't just that new details might emerge with the subtlety and fidelity of the reproduction (though they hopefully will), but that the book may invite a different sort of attention than the image projected on the screen.

Art books are among the most expensive additions a library can make to its collection, and it is understandable that they often remain among the least developed sections. However, there are multiple ways to seek out art images online. Navigating museum collections within those institutions' websites themselves is one habit librarians should encourage, since different filtering options will be available than those provided by search engines. Websites geared to potential buyers, like LiveAuctioneers, Artsy, or Sotheby's, along with those of specific galleries, may also be of use. The obvious upside to the availability of digital information about art is that living in a large metropolitan area is much less of a prerequisite for knowing what sorts of shows and exhibitions are going up. Print and digital sites like *Artforum, Frieze, Art in America, Mousse,* and *Hyperallergic* include listings of notable exhibitions, alongside longer reviews and commentary for national and international shows. Digital access does have a downside, however, since many libraries will be priced out of access to extensive and high-quality collections, such as the Artstor Digital Library, which requires steep membership fees. Other collections, like that of the Museum of Modern Art, offer only limited access for nonmembers. In any case, getting hold of the strongest reproduction of an image is partially analogous to getting the best version of any other form of information. Because subtlety and detail count quite a bit, interlibrary loans might be a strong access option.

Finally, it's useful to note that the complexities and limitations inherent in an artwork's reproducibility have generated their own body of literature. Librarians and patrons looking to consider the wider implications of reproduction might consult Walter Benjamin's landmark essay "The Work of Art in the Age of Mechanical Reproduction" (1936) or Andre Malraux's more upbeat *The Museum without Walls* (1949) as a way into some of these issues.

THE BIGGER PICTURE

We have directed much attention in this chapter to how writers engage with art, rather than the modes of researching art and art histories. We want to conclude with a few words about how this emphasis responds to broad trends in research on art, and offer a few titles that might provide a context for those who are newly grappling with either subject. As a generalist librarian working with writers who are interested in art, it may be useful to conceptualize art as a field with divisions beyond those of genre and style. A conversation with a librarian whose collection supports an art museum revealed, for instance, that she responds to questions of provenance, value, and object history far more often than ones about artistic movements or traditions. This distinction may prove useful to librarians who need to know what information a writing patron seeks, since the former type of query involves the scrutiny of auction and exhibition catalogs, while the latter can be satisfied with books on art history and other secondary sources.

The resources available for this research are extensive and vary with time period, medium, and more. A few resources that many libraries are likely to have on hand can satisfy some queries before turning referrals to more specialized collections or interlibrary loan. One database that can be helpful in understanding an artist's biography and professional trajectory, and offer insights into her philosophy of creation, is Gale's *Contemporary Authors* (https://www.gale.com/c/contemporary-authors-online). If an artist, like Georgia O'Keeffe, has written about her art or about the subject more generally, then that person may be classified as an author and included in the database. Given the encompassing nature of *Contemporary Authors* entries, with bibliographies of primary and secondary source matter, they represent a valuable and often easily accessible source of information. The articles in *Wikipedia, Encyclopedia Britannica,* and other encyclopedias may also be useful for essential details like the relationships between artists and their contemporaries, whether a figure is associated with a particular school or movement, and chronologies of their works. It is also useful to remain aware of the many specialized encyclopedias and handbooks associated with this field and its subdivisions that can provide perspectives on everything from comics to movies.

Finally, a book like *The Story of Art* (1995) represents a compendium of media, movements, and notable artists. Its author, Ernst Gombrich, was known for his readable narratives that explain subjects involving both incredible detail and wide-ranging scope. More recently, Victoria Finlay has written *Color: A Natural History of the Palette* (2002) to focus attention more intently on the way different artists and eras have produced the colors which characterize famous works of art. We mention these two books as examples of nontechnical works that aspire, fully and genuinely, to engage the general reader. Thus, they stand not only as sources of information, but as models of writing about works of art.

Notes

1. William Carlos Williams, "Landscape with the Fall of Icarus," poets.org, Academy of American Poets, https://www.poets.org/poetsorg/poem/landscape-fall-icarus; and W. H. Auden, "Musée des Beaux Arts," "Paintings

& Poems" class, Emory University Department of English, http://english
.emory.edu/classes/paintings&poems/auden.html.

2. Angela Chen, "Poet Robin Coste Lewis: 'I Am an Artist through to My
Marrow,'" *The Guardian* (December 21, 2015), https://www.theguardian.com/
books/2015/dec/21/robin-coste-lewis-poetry-voyage-of-the-sable-venus.

3. Tisa Bryant, *Unexplained Presence* (Leon Works, 2007), ix–x.

4. See "Helen Levitt," Art & Artists, Museum of Modern Art, https://www
.moma.org/artists/3520.

5. James Elkins, *What Painting Is* (New York: Routledge, 2004), 87.

6. See "Spiders," Louise Bourgeois: The Complete Prints & Books, Museum of
Modern Art, https://www.moma.org/explore/collection/lb/themes/spiders;
and "Grids," Guggenheim Museum, https://www.guggenheim.org/arts
-curriculum/topic/grids#_edn14.

7. Tomas Unger, "Teju Cole's Incantations," The Millions (June 13, 2017),
https://themillions.com/2017/06/tk-4.html.

8. Jennifer Burek Pierce, "Grassroots Report: Checking Out Art in the
Heartland," *American Libraries* 36, no. 9 (October 2005): 75.

5

Occupations

During the Great Recession of 2008–2009, literary critics perceived a crisis: unlike fiction writers of the Great Depression of the 1930s, hardly anyone was writing about labor and the world of work. Their concern came in waves. In spring 2009 Judith Flanders asked, "Why don't novels 'do' work?"[1] By the following January, the novelist John Lanchester concurred that "the world of work, especially of modern work, is significantly under-represented in fiction."[2] Two months later, Jennifer Schuessler followed up with her own jab:

> Joblessness may be hovering around 10 percent, with some 29 million Americans out of work or searching for full-time employment, but there's one group of people whose persistent alienation from regular employment has emerged as a particularly serious problem. I refer, of course, to novelists.[3]

Was such an omission really possible? Had novelists become unconcerned with the world of work? Were they, as Schuessler alleges, alienated from it? Or were their commentaries more reflective of the fact that whereas, in the 1930s, the Works Project Administration had supported the professional activities of writers and dramatists, their livelihoods were not aided by more recent federal recovery programs? Whether the case made by Flanders and others is literally true, it was clear that the Great Recession, like the Great Depression before it, had made readers and critics hungry for representation of the world of work that occupies most of our adult lives.

Work is a subject, after all, that has historically filled volumes, from the Bible to children's books, to poetry, well into the twentieth century, when we consider the Detroit verse of Philip Levine and David Lee's *Porcine Canticles* (1984). Modern novels that feature work, whether the academics and industrialists in David Lodge's *Nice Work* (1988), the preacher who pursues his vocation as he faces death in Marilynne Robinson's *Gilead* (2005), or the cavalierly malicious and inept fence-builders in Magnus Mills's *The Restraint of Beasts* (1998), have won critical notice. A book like Joshua Ferris's *Then We Came to the End* (2007) is the exception that proves the rule: a widely acclaimed realist novel that is focused on contemporary office work. Whether the criticisms of how contemporary writing represents the world of work are valid is best understood in the context of a longer and broader tradition. Thus, we turn to examples of the ways that varied literary genres have engaged the subject of employment, and the avenues for researching the conditions of work, as well as the question of making a living as a writer.

As Tolstoy said, "One can live magnificently in this world if one knows how to work and how to love."[4] The topic of love has whole genres and poetic forms dedicated to it. The topic of work, however, feels less formally tangible in the world of letters until we are reminded of its many facets, and its differences across time and genre. Certainly, its historic traces are probably different from the lot of contemporary working adult Americans, who spend half their waking, weekday lives in the practice of their occupations; that is, if they're lucky enough to secure and survive on a single full-time job. Recent research has documented how many people are holding down multiple jobs, and this fact alone may anchor present-day narratives that reckon with the limitations of the uneven economic recovery that followed the Great Recession.

The word *occupation,* with its synonyms *job* or *career,* also intersects with the words *vocation* and *profession.* The latter two terms suggest, respectively, activities we are *called* to do (vocation, from *vox,* meaning "voice") or identify with (*profession,* as in what we profess to be). The tasks we do for wages every day might not actually be our calling or profession. Many of us find ourselves in occupational activities by chance; often, career narratives involve "falling into" a line of work rather than consciously choosing or pursuing it. Nor are many of our occupations near the core of how we identify as persons. A look at bios on Librarian Twitter will reveal a "book lover" or "cat person" for every "information specialist," for instance. Moreover, the idea of *occupations* becomes more inclusive than vocations or professions when we truly open it up to the activities that *occupy* us in various ways, whether or not these activities are a means of economic support. Much more occupies our time, thoughts, and energies than the things we do in exchange for money.

Nevertheless, the tasks we perform for fiscal remuneration do indeed occupy a great deal of who we are, from our bodies to our emotional states and even our dreams. Robert Hass's *Time and Materials,* winner of the 2008 Pulitzer Prize in Poetry, opens with a two-line poem about the dreams of farmers, titled "Iowa, January": "In the long winter nights, a farmer's dreams are narrow. / Over and over, he enters the furrow."[5] For an Iowa farmer, the winter months are a time for planning and purchasing rather than planting and harvesting, yet Hass has this farmer's work occupying his imagination out of season. Hass's rhythmically dizzying second line puts his reader in the farmer's winter fever dream, bearing in mind the rhythms of the work—planting and harvesting row by row, or working according to the rhythm of the seasons. Perhaps one definition of an occupation would be the thing a person cannot help but dream within himself, even in winter, when the activity has ceased.

Talking, Listening, and Work

Studs Terkel's *Working: People Talk about What They Do All Day and How They Feel about What They Do* (1974) is a landmark work of oral history on the subject of labor. It is an achievement that also poses a question like the ones that opened this chapter: why are there not more books like this? How did it come to be that working, the thing that most people spend most of their waking lives doing, is *not* actually something we read and hear more about? We can use Terkel's legacy as a starting point for considering how writing about work belongs to both library settings and to the patrons who use them.

The first way to do this is simply to mimic Terkel by asking patrons to write about their own work lives. You can consult or pass out photocopies of text from *Working* in order to illustrate a general point: the actual details of a job are often more interesting to hear about than the person doing the job thinks they are. It is particularly important to emphasize that these jobs don't have to be glamorous or recognized by the wider culture as particularly vital or compelling. Workers have a specialized, insider knowledge about their jobs, but they also have a highly subjective way of experiencing the challenges, surprises, and boredom that are entailed with any kind of work.

You may narrow the prompt, asking participants to write about their first job, their favorite or least favorite job, or one they wish they had or the one they hope never to do. You might want to widen the scope of the question by considering unwaged labor (housework, child-rearing, internships, homework, chores) or work they do just for pleasure.

Alternatively, you can ask patrons to pair up and interview one another about their work lives. If you know you have several sessions, you might assign participants to interview one or more people they know on the topic. Discussions about oral history methodology have the potential to complicate this slightly, though this particular form of investigation and conversation also has the potential to introduce an accessible and empowering form of research and community-building.

As much as they fill our imaginations, the jobs we do also occupy our bodies. This becomes evident when reading the physical descriptions of characters and subjects in prose and poetry, since the occupations of our bodies informs our physical appearance. In Victorian fiction, a chimney sweep is besooted, small, and short. More physically demanding occupations make for more muscular characters. Occupations in what some now call the "knowledge economy" might mean something very different from those that involve physical or manual labor.

A more specific example, mentioned in other chapters, emerges in Muriel Rukeyser's long poem "The Book of the Dead." This poem reveals how one of the miners, Mearl Blankenship, contracted silicosis through his work digging a tunnel. Rukeyser writes:

> He stood against the rock
> facing the river
> grey river grey face
> the rock mottled behind him
> like X-ray plate enlarged
> diffuse and stony
> his face against the stone.
>
> J C Dunbar said that I was the very picture of health
> when I went to Work at that tunnel.[6]

In this passage, Rukeyser compares Blankenship's body to the natural resources against which it is set and with which he works. He takes on the appearance of the rock—the mottling of the rock models his very insides, ruined by the disease he has contracted by mining it. Standing against the river, he becomes the color of the river, his aspect made grey by his condition, which he contracted from an industrial project initiated to manipulate the river. His face is "stony" against the stone. Blankenship's body has become its labor unto death, a tragedy made apparent by Rukeyser's figurative X-ray that sets up the distressful irony in the next stanza: that he was once "the very *picture* of health." In short, Rukeyser asks, do we become the very picture of our labors? Writers contemporary with Rukeyser seemed to think so, since in the wake of the Great Depression, the popular imagination was populated not only with the emaciated bodies of impoverished tenant farmers and industrial workers, but also with the image of the "fat capital-ist," like the crooked banker Henry Gatewood in John Ford's film *Stagecoach* (1939).

The labor that occupies our bodies also affects our emotional states. Few American writers have been as occupationally minded as Herman Melville, whose scrivener Bartleby refuses to copy, whose steamboat in *The Confidence-Man* is practically a vocational *Who's Who,* and whose monomaniacal whaler Captain Ahab is so consumed by his occupation that he leads his whole ship to ruin in revenge-hunting an unattainable white whale. Indeed, Melville's novels *Redburn* (1849), *White-Jacket* (1850), and *Moby-Dick* (1851) are a virtual compendium of life aboard sailing vessels in the mid-nineteenth century. In *Moby-Dick,* before the *Pequod's* fateful final confrontation with Moby Dick, Melville has revealed friendship, intimacy, and community among its sailors. Literature provides examples, then, of how occupations fill us with despair and joy, en-liven us, and sometimes destroy us. Our labors can both connect us to others and enrapture us as individuals.

Like Melville, Walt Whitman was preoccupied with occupa-tions. In Whitman's "Song of Joys," his speaker sings of engineers, motherhood, fishermen, manhood, and womanhood. He also penned "A Song for Occupations," and his exploratory medley of the American self, "Song of Myself," is likewise rife with allusions to the personae of everyday American laborers, some of these devel-oped from archival source-texts. As Ed Folsom notes of section 34, the so-called "Alamo section" of "Song of Myself," which is actu-ally about the Mexican War massacre at Goliad, "recent discoveries indicate that Whitman may well have derived this description of the massacre from the journal of a Mexican officer who was witness to the events."[7] Elsewhere in the poem, Whitman's account of a fire-man can be traced to a contemporaneous newspaper passage, as can his Civil War poem "Cavalry Crossing a Ford." Rather than arising from Romantic visions of the nation, these poems reflect research using what we now call primary sources. Whitman's employment of primary source-texts suggests that writers should hit the stacks or peruse periodicals to furnish a scene with employment details beyond their experiences.

It's not just in his poetry that Whitman appropriates such information. Daneen Wardrop writes in "Civil War Nursing Narratives: Whitman's Memoranda during the War and Eroticism" that one of Whitman's most enduring pieces of prose—his memoir about his time as a makeshift war nurse caring for wounded soldiers, including his brother, at Armory Square Hospital—was largely inspired by the nursing narratives that preceded it.[8] Nursing narratives became very popular after Florence Nightingale's labors in the Crimean War, and women's participation as nurses in the U.S. Civil War captured the popular imagination. Louisa May Alcott, who herself worked briefly as a nurse in the Union Hotel Hospital in Washington, DC, an experience she semi-fictionalizes in *Hospital Sketches,* begins her longer novel, *Work,* with her protagonist Christie's wish to be "a Florence Nightingale" (6). Like Florence Nightingale, Christie, as "an army nurse who had done well" (427), uses her experience as a war nurse to earn a national spotlight, which also aided Alcott's own authority and renown. For those to whom the soldier's narrative was off-limits (namely women, though also perhaps the middle-aged Whitman), the nurse's narrative availed.

The trick for writers is to make the occupations in their creative works as thematically important as those of Whitman and Alcott. For them, the occupation of war nursing was the perfect vehicle for their respective projects. Whitman as a writer aimed to be the nation's "Wound-Dresser," suturing the national wounds left by the Civil War, and Alcott used nursing to garner authority for women. More recently, Lin-Manual Miranda has adapted the *Hamilton* lyrics proclaiming, "Immigrants, we get the job done," to comment on recent immigration policy and the economic plight of the often undocumented people who provide the essential but little-recognized labor that underpins the U.S. economy.[9] Beyond the question of how to locate details of practice and other elements of authenticity, the more substantial issue writers must consider is why a character works. Writers must focus their attention beyond issues of familiarity or convenience and confront the larger questions about what work accomplishes and what it means to do particular kinds of work.

BOOKS ABOUT MEDICAL OCCUPATIONS

- *And the Band Played On: Politics, People, and the AIDS Epidemic,* Randy Shilts (1987)
- *Arrowsmith,* Sinclair Lewis (1925)
- *A Case of Need,* Michael Crichton (1993)
- *A Fortunate Man: The Story of a Country Doctor,* John Berger (1967)
- *The Children's Hospital,* Chris Adrian (2007)
- *The Cider House Rules,* John Irving (1985)
- *Complications: A Surgeon's Notes on an Imperfect Science,* Atul Gawande (2003)
- *The Empathy Exams,* Leslie Jamison (2014)
- *The Healing Art: A Doctor's Black Bag of Poetry,* Rafael Campo (2003)
- *Heirs of General Practice,* John McPhee (1984)
- *Hospital,* Julie Salamon (2009)
- *House of God,* Samuel Shem (2008)
- *The Intern Blues,* Robert Marion (2001)
- *Intern: A Doctor's Initiation,* Sandeep Jauhar (2008)
- *Middlemarch,* George Eliot (1872)
- *The Emperor of All Maladies: A Biography of Cancer,* Siddhartha Mukherjee (2010)
- *The Immortal Life of Henrietta Lacks,* Rebecca Skloot (2010)
- *The Midwife of Hope River,* Patricia Harman (2012)
- *Mortal Lessons,* Richard Selzer (1976)
- *Outlander,* Diana Gabaldon (1992)
- *Poetry in Medicine: An Anthology of Poems about Doctors, Patients, Illness and Healing,* ed. Michael Salcman and Michael Collier (2015)
- *Saturday,* Ian McEwan (2005)
- *The Spirit Catches You and You Fall Down,* Anne Fadiman (1997)
- *This Side of Doctoring: Reflections from Women in Medicine,* Eliza Lo Chin (2001)
- *When Breath Becomes Air,* Paul Kalanithi (2016)

Many occupations not only have built-in resonances but whole genres associated with them. Consider the importance of the detective or private eye in noir or crime fiction; the cowboy, the rancher, the lawman, or the hired gun in the western; the scientists and engineers in science fiction; the socialite in the comedy of manners; the homemaker in the family melodrama; and the wizard in fantasy. And while many of the occupations associated with genre fiction are *real* occupations in the *real* world, often the mandates of the genre call for different balances of imagination and research, and different kinds of research at that. While the private eye of detective fiction may be solving a murder, he doesn't do this in the same way that a detective in true crime fiction does it. Thus research for noir might have more to do with taking notes of lingo from past books, rather than chain of custody procedures from contemporary legal manuals.

 ## Science Fiction

For this activity, you may begin by having your writing group read a science fiction narrative of your choosing. Sources for the selection include issues of *Asimov's Science Fiction,* one of the leading Anglophone science fiction journals, or a story from *Asimov's* made available on the author's website: "The New Mother" by Eugene Fischer, which appeared in 2015 (https://medium .com/@glorioushubris/the-new-mother-9df848da415b). Discuss the various occupations in the story and how they intersect with the new or speculative science and technologies of the text. Is there a scientist or physician in the story? What kind of science or medicine does she practice? Is her occupation related to the new or speculative technologies of the narrative? What social implications do these new sciences have? In "The New Mother," for instance, Fischer interrogates how families and societies are organized around reproduction by speculating how the social fabric might change if women were able to reproduce asexually.

After a brief discussion, have your writing group create science fiction narratives of their own, beginning with a concept (like reproduction, in Fischer's case) and working from there. Other, related activities include the following:

▓ Is there a concept, law, phenomenon, or social issue that interests your writers? Have them jot down several ideas. These might be marriage, health care inequality, climate change, animal rights, or others. As an example, we'll use animal rights.

▓ What is the current state of that concept or issue? That is, describe the current state of animal rights.

▓ What is a science or technology whose advent could fundamentally change that state? For instance, if one animal species could attain the ability to communicate effectively with humans, how would humans' relationship with these animals change? What would that new society look like?

▓ What is the setting of your narrative? This involves thinking temporally as well as geographically. Is it in a near distant earth, or a distant past earth? Or is it in a galaxy far, far away?

▓ What do the occupations look like that involve your speculative science or technology? List five, as well as their primary responsibilities.

▓ Choose one of these occupations for your protagonist, and write your narrative. A few questions you might ask writers to consider are: What are the fundamental differences between the society of your narrative and the society we live in today? How does your protagonist negotiate her world differently from you and yours?

Occupations need not be real in our world to be real in fiction. J. K. Rowling went to great pains to map out the occupational economies of her wizarding world in the *Harry Potter* series. Unlike in Tolkien's *Lord of the Rings,* Rowling's wizard isn't an occupation unto himself. Rowling staffs her world with administrative wizards in the Ministry of Magic, pedagogical wizards who teach classes at Hogwarts, law-enforcing wizards known as Aurors, journalist wizards with magical note-taking devices, beast-keeping wizards, and so on. Rowling's world illustrates as well as any how directly related occupations are to world-building. As your patrons begin to write about occupations, they should keep in mind not only their chosen occupations' relationship to the literature that came before it, but also how that occupation fits in to the society and economy of a well-imagined world. It should be noted that even Rowling's wizards couldn't create money or food, which kept them situated in economic relation to one another.

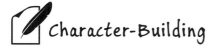 ## Character-Building

Whether your patrons are writing about the real world or a speculative one, authenticating details can make that world feel more fully realized. In these activities, your writing group will imagine character-building details centered on the specifics of an occupation, either real or imagined.

- First, assign each patron an occupation. These can be brainstormed as a group and then claimed by volunteers, or each individual can choose their own. Alternatively, if your group is feeling adventurous, you may have them draw occupations out of a hat. These can range from hyper-specialized occupations to traditional ones to speculative ones, from best boy grip on a movie set to physician to wizard. These will be the occupations for a main character.

- Next, each writer should research or imagine the tools and instruments needed for her occupation. After enumerating these tools, each patron in your writing group should choose one tool. For that tool, your writers should list four past, momentous occasions when that tool was used. If the writer's occupation is physician, for instance, the tool might be a stethoscope, and you would need to imagine four momentous scenes in which your character has used that stethoscope during her career. This will give your tool a symbolic freight or emotional charge. Then your writers are to feature that tool in a newly written scene.

- What is everyone's character doing at 3:23 P.M. on a Thursday in October? Have your patrons write a scene at precisely that time, informed by their research or imagining of their occupations' daily routines. If you'd like to take the activity further, you may use the same time for four different days of the year: What is the character doing at 3:23 P.M. on September 21, December 21, March 21, and June 21? Your participants may produce four scenes.

- Write page 18 of the employee handbook your character was given on her first day on the job. Then write a scene in which that page is referenced.

- What is your character's typical workday wardrobe? Describe the contents of her closet and laundry hamper. Write a scene in which she's late for work, but she's out of clean laundry.
- Write your character's résumé.
- Chart your character's financial status. Does she have student debt? A mortgage? How much? What is her yearly take-home pay? What does she pay in taxes? Does she have a retirement plan? Health insurance? How much did she pay for her car? How much is in her bank account? Use this information to write a scene in which your character argues with someone about finances.

Some occupations in genre fiction, such as noir's private eye or the ratiocinative investigator of detective fiction (for example, Sherlock Holmes), help propel the plots of their narratives through an activity with which librarians should be acutely familiar: information-seeking. For murder mysteries, especially, or whodunits with aha! moments as their critical plot junctures, information-seeking occupies a great deal of the protagonists' time and mental energies at the same time that it advances the plot through moments of revelation. Many genre narratives are structured by concealing a *plot behind the plot,* or a scheme that has been set before the narrative begins. It's the job of the information-seeker to reveal this scheme over time. The private eye unravels the scheme that induces his client, typically a femme fatale, to enlist his services in the first place. The detective not only solves the murder but articulates the motives, machinations, and social forces behind it.

Information-seeking behavior is also very important in horror fiction when initially unexplainable, supernatural forces are at play. Sometimes the protagonist of horror fiction even enlists the assistance of a library or librarian. Other times they perform simple web searches to contextualize the supernatural phenomena they are experiencing. Questions are asked of local folklore experts, and demonology texts are consulted. Regardless of the particular manifestation of the information-seeking behavior, it provides genre writers with ready-made occupations and activities around which to center their plot as a slow series of exposures that add up to a larger puzzle. In Dan Brown's *The Da Vinci Code* (2003), for instance, the protagonist, Robert Langdon, is a Harvard scholar of symbols—the very things that must be deciphered in order to unravel the mystery of a museum curator's murder that initiates the plot. Aided by a cryptologist love interest, Langdon seeks information, symbol by symbol, until it leads him not only to the curator's murderer, but also to the revelation of the Holy Grail. Brown could well have made Langdon and his partner curious clergy, art historians, or even dauntless journalists or graduate students. Langdon's credentials as a secular Harvard professor who is set against religious antagonists also make the book—like the Sherlock Holmes narratives that debunk local superstitions through inductive reasoning and research—an Enlightenment narrative. Thus, while the occupation of information-seeking comes in many forms, the writer should consider other valences the particular occupations may bear. For authenticating details, writers will need to research the precise means of information-seeking that are available to each occupation.

For contemporary occupations, the best one-stop shop for the particulars of any occupation is the Bureau of Labor Statistics' *Occupational Outlook Handbook* (www.bls.gov/ooh). The digital version of the OOH is a database of occupations that provides a summary of "Quick Facts" for each listed job, such as median pay, entry-level education required, and how fast the job is expected to grow in the near future. The entries also contain brief descriptions of work environments and job responsibilities. Other reference sources for contemporary occupations include:

- the subscription database *Vocational Biographies* (www.vocbio.com)
- *The Encyclopedia of Careers and Vocational Guidance*
- the subscription database *Ferguson's Career Guidance Center*
- Ferguson's companion *Careers in Focus* series
- select trade publications like the *American Journal of Nursing Career Guide* and *Successful Farming*

If your patrons are looking for information about occupations in or from the past and your library doesn't possess relevant resources, more and more digitized archives are being made available online. While Louisa May Alcott and Walt Whitman could draw on their life experiences as nurses (or as a would-be nurse in Whitman's case) to depict hospital scenes, contemporary authors might visit online repositories of the *Armory Square Hospital Gazette,* which can be found in the "Newspapers" section of the Civil War Washington website (http://civilwardc.org/texts/newspapers/). Civil War Washington also collects digitized letters from soldiers and medical cases drawn from *The Medical and Surgical History of the War of the Rebellion.* One might also peruse the digital holdings of the National Archives, both those of the United States and the United Kingdom. The latter, for instance, has a whole collection devoted to nineteenth-century prison ships, including a ship surgeon's log (www.nationalarchives.gov.uk/education/resources/19th-century -prison-ships/). If, like Herman Melville, your patron is interested in whaling narratives, you might send her to the New Bedford Whaling Museum's website, which has a digitized archive of logbooks and journals (https://www.whalingmuseum.org/explore/ library/logbooks-journals). If your patrons are interested in African-Americans' labor conditions under slavery, they may visit the Library of Congress's online collection "Born in Slavery: Slave Narratives from the Federal Writers' Project, 1936–1938," which contains more than 2,300 first-person accounts and more than 500 photographs (https://www.loc.gov/collections/slave-narratives-from -the-federal-writers-project-1936-to-1938/about-this-collection/).

Even if your patrons write about occupations from personal experience, they may have trouble recollecting details from their own lives without research. Your patrons may be working on memoirs that revolve around their previous occupations, or they may be taking up social media's #FirstSevenJobs hashtag challenge, in which they describe their first seven paying jobs. More than likely, if you work at a public or university library, you'll have patrons working on personal narratives or goal statements for admission to professional schools. In any case, it's to the patron's advantage

PROFESSIONAL SCHOOLS AND PERSONAL STATEMENTS

Personal statements for entry into professional programs such as medical school or law school aim to bridge an applicant's previous experience with his or her newly intended vocation. In addition to performing the research outlined above for vocational reference, the patron may need your help in envisioning how to begin writing such a statement. Statements written by candidates who have been admitted to programs have taken many forms, and admissions officers will tell you that there is no one formula for a compelling essay that will command their attention.

It is important to think of admissions officers as the audience for such essays. Regardless of whether admissions officers have a background in the field whose degree program they support, these statements typically should be devoid of professional jargon. This is to say, admissions officers should be considered a lay audience without an assumed specialized knowledge of your patron's aspirational field. Admissions officers do read for a living, and they particularly read a lot of personal statements, so perfunctory responses miss the opportunity for your patron to stand out in a stack of essays. Here are a few activities to suggest:

- For each of your patron's work and volunteer experiences, ask her to describe a contribution she made to those positions that only she could have made.
- Alternately, advise her to begin brainstorming by outlining five moments that truly changed her way of thinking. Through a process of drafting and revision, she may be able to translate these episodes into an honest essay that persuades admissions officers that she would be a welcome addition to an incoming class, providing a unique perspective and skill set and possessing a voice that recommends her.

If your patron is looking for concrete examples, plenty of essays that have successfully resulted in professional school admission can be found on the Web, using search terms such as "sample personal statements" combined with "medical school."

to consider the archives and artifacts she might well have kept of herself. If your patron is digitally inclined, she might have archived e-mails for and about work that are accessible through simple text-string searches under "All Mail" or the 'Search Mail' search bar. It helps to think of a strategic word to search for that would recover key messages, whether this word denotes a core activity, a client, or a document. Digital searches of personal archives could also extend to your patron's social media accounts. It's difficult to recover Tweets more than two years old, but on Facebook, one may click on one's profile and then on "Activity Log" to evoke a search bar that can access one's entire history on the platform. For the non-digitally inclined patron, artifacts such as tax returns and pay stubs may prove useful, as may old employment handbooks or training manuals.

AUTHORIAL PURSUITS

In the end, your more writerly patrons may aspire to college and graduate programs in creative writing or to careers in creative writing. Creative writing, though, is a profession whose ladder to success often seems hidden to all but a few. The *Occupational Outlook Handbook* has an entry for "Writers and Authors," though it conflates creative writers with other kinds of content writers like advertising copywriters. The path to financial success for a creative writer, one who dictates one's own content and materials, is as precarious as it is mysterious and depends on a great many gatekeepers, not the least of whom are reading audiences themselves. Unless one self-publishes, to arrive at a potential reading audience typically requires an agent and an editor, or in the case of poets, editors and contest judges. When aspiring writers approach you with requests for information about turning their interests into a career, you might begin with the following information and resources.

The truth is that creative writing in and of itself is not a remunerative career, unless one is Stephen King, J. K. Rowling, or some other best-selling author. Even Pulitzer Prize winners in fiction receive much of their income (not to mention health insurance) from university teaching. Parlaying your talents in a literary genre into classroom work, however, requires a master of fine arts degree and a nationally distributed book published by a reputable press. Others who have found prestige through book publication might eke out a living by freelance journalism or by writing screenplays for the movies or television. However, the vast majority of creative writers, even at the height of their profession, do not receive sufficient income from their publications alone to afford the mainstays of middle-class life. The novelist Tony Tulathimutte outlines "Four 'Types' of Creative Writing 'Careers'" (scare quotes his) rather humorously for *Catapult* magazine, where he enumerates models for sustainable writing careers, from faculty work to freelancing.[10] For the determined, Tom Kealey's *Creative Writing MFA Handbook: A Guide for Prospective Graduate Students* (2008) will take your patrons through the ins and outs of applying for graduate programs (many of them fully funded) in creative writing.

If you'd like to get your patrons started in submitting their work for publication, there are various resources for publishing poems and short stories. The annually published resource book *Writer's Market* is a must-have for any library, and if your collection budget will support it, you might also purchase its more specialized siblings, *Novel & Short Story Writer's Market* and *Poet's Market*. Even if your patron-writers don't go on to become independently wealthy as authors, they are likely to appreciate the library's support in either researching the careers of their characters or researching the possibilities in their own writing vocation.

Perhaps your patron is researching writing careers precisely because she's committing one of the crimes that are often articulated by the critics: writing about writers. Writing, after all, is its own occupation with its own concomitant materials and activities, and as the aforementioned critics could tell you, it's not an underexplored genre. William Luce's one-woman play *The Belle of Amherst* (1976) brought to active life the previously static image of Emily Dickinson. Many of Stephen King's characters are writers, and that famous task-shirker Bartleby, of course, was a scribe. One suspects that critics' aversion to writers writing about writing has more to do with the lack of occupational diversity in the upper echelons of literary publishing than it does with the idea that it can't be or hasn't been done well. To do it well, one must merely follow the same strategies for animating a persona or character from any occupation: begin with research for familiarity and authenticating details as we've suggested above, and then imagine beyond it.

Notes

1. Judith Flanders, "Why Don't Novels 'Do' Work?" *The Guardian* (March 30, 2009), https://www.theguardian.com/books/booksblog/2009/mar/30/work -novels-fiction-flanders.

2. John Lanchester, "When Fiction Breaks Down," *The Telegraph* (January 29, 2010), https://www.telegraph.co.uk/culture/books/7093699/When-fiction -breaks-down.html.

3. Jennifer Schuessler, "Take This Job and Write It," *New York Times Book Review* (March 11, 2010), https://www.nytimes.com/2010/03/14/books/review/ Schuessler-t.html.

4. Henri Troyat, *Tolstoy* (Grove, 2001), 158.

5. Robert Hass, *Time and Materials: Poems 1997–2005* (New York: HarperCollins, 2007), 1.

6. Muriel Rukeyser, *Out of Silence: Selected Poems* (Evanston, IL: Northwestern University Press, 1994), 18.

7. Walt Whitman, with Ed Folsom and Christopher Merrill, *Song of Myself: With a Complete Commentary* (University of Iowa Press, 2016), 119.

8. Daneen Wardrop, "Civil War Nursing Narratives: Whitman's Memoranda during the War and Eroticism," *Walt Whitman Quarterly Review* 23, no. 1 (2005): 3.

9. "The Hamilton Mixtape: Immigrants (We Get the Job Done)," in *Hamilton: An American Musical* (June 28, 2017), https://www.youtube.com/watch?v=6 _35a7sn6ds.

10. Tony Tulathimutte, "Four 'Types' of Creative Writing 'Careers,'" *Catapult* (May 24, 2017), https://catapult.co/stories/the-four-types-of-creative-writing -careers.

6

Taking Measures

SCIENTIFIC AND TECHNICAL SUBJECTS

What last sent you looking for information about a health condition or a new medication? What was it like, the last time you paged through a technical manual or even a set of instructions for rendering a new piece of technology, a television or a computer, workable in your daily life? What inspired you when you last tried a new recipe? Was it the author's voice, tempting photos, or a discussion of how an ingredient emerged from a particular place? How often do you rely on maps, whether printed ones or the tiny, handheld versions now found on the screens of our phones? Have you consulted a book to see whether a garden plant would attract butterflies or thrive in your local climate? Did you consult an app to replay a bird song or to compare the color of feathers to ones you've just noticed and not recognized? When did you last check the time? Each of these ordinary instances reflects our daily, often unconscious involvement with science and technology.

The effects of science, technology, and medicine permeate the world we live in and may be equally present in our writing about the world. Traces of these topics appear across genres, although the treatment and depth of expression vary in the hands of different authors. A writer need not be categorized as a scientific or technical writer in order to draw, considerably and skillfully, on details derived from scientific study.

Writers might draw on knowledge of science, technology, and medicine for any number of reasons. Is a character afflicted by a health condition that controls the plot, as we've seen in popular novels ranging from *Love Story* (1970) to *The Fault in Our Stars* (2012)? Does the plot hang on a projected technological innovation that stems from contemporary scientific knowledge, whether in classics like the novels of Jules Verne or the more recent *Jurassic Park* (1990)? Is the author reconstructing the lives of people who were involved in yet not credited with significant innovations, as recounted in *Bombshell: The Hedy Lamarr Story* (2017) or *Hidden Figures* (2016)? Even the most mundane facts of daily life involve science. Cooking relies on chemistry, but so does poison, and both allow writers to build and reroute their narratives. Weather, which can be the menacing centerpiece of a work like *The Perfect Storm* (1997), or serve as a picturesque backdrop, as in the eighteenth-century Frost Fairs held on the River Thames that feature briefly in Virginia Woolf's *Orlando* (1928), has been recorded as scientific data for more than a century. Data about weather patterns is currently provided by the National Oceanic and Atmospheric Administration, while the British Library preserves contemporary illustrations that depict the ways people responded to weather conditions.[1]

While some writers invent details—in John Green's novel *The Fault in Our Stars* (2012), for example, he includes a note cautioning readers that Phalanxafor, the drug that produces Hazel's "miracle," is fictitious—others, like Andy Weir, author of the wildly popular, self-published 2011 novel *The Martian,* rely on their own scientific education and continued research to imbue a fictional world with as much realism as possible. Thus, as we guide writers toward resources that can structure their stories, we must consider whether they seek information on what is possible or what might be plausible. Using follow-up questions in reference interactions with writers will be essential in determining our responses to their technical queries. Does a writer need, for example, a clear sense of what a clinical trial is, or is she interested in actual, current experimental treatment mechanisms?[2]

We can see a number of these elements embedded in a novel like Curtis Sittenfeld's *Sisterland* (2013). On the surface, *Sisterland* is about the bonds between twins. Its narrator seems determined to defy the genetic and familial connections with her sister, but this is only the starting point for a story that asks readers and characters alike to grapple with the nature and the limits of knowledge. While the book depends in part on the reader's understanding of inherited genetic traits, the tensions between laboratory science and psychic prediction are crucial to its plot. Even its depiction of the nature of motherhood, of trying to decide when a child's illness warrants emergency medical care, grapples with what we can perceive and what we must entrust to experts and diagnostic technologies. *Sisterland* stands, then, in the company of other, more obviously science-oriented stories that have captured readers' attention in recent years.

Two more recent works demonstrate the ways that science and technology anchor popular and appealing writing. Anthony Doerr's Pulitzer Prize-winning novel *All the Light We Cannot See* (2014) centers on the historical development of technology and tools that are integral to the pursuit of war and resistance. In its early pages, Marie-Laure reads Jules Verne's *Twenty Thousand Leagues under the Sea* (1870), and the means of receiving radio transmissions figure throughout the book. Doerr begins the story with "a scene of leaflets warning civilians of the oncoming artillery. The airplanes heard but not yet seen, like the depths of the ocean described in Verne's pages, stretch the parameters of the character's and reader's perception simultaneously.[3] A recent nonfiction bestseller, *Astrophysics for People in a Hurry* (2017), endeavors to make complex and technical explanations of the universe accessible to those who lack the author's knowledge and expert background. Its author, Neil deGrasse Tyson, is an impassioned advocate for scientific understanding as essential to navigating the world and being more alive to its wonders, and he offers readers—and other writers—a model for how to share ideas derived from years of study with people who are unfamiliar with these concepts. One reviewer has observed the outrageously evocative details in Tyson's explanatory analogies: "To imagine the density of a pulsar, think about stuffing a hundred-million elephants into a ChapStick casing."[4] These recent bestsellers suggest why writers pursue scientific topics for general audiences: the scientific and technical material enhances our perspective on what is possible, and on how precarious or contingent certain aspects of life may be. These titles can also suggest potential approaches to incorporating science into the work that writers share with the world.

Although it may seem most natural to think of the role of science and technology in genres like science fiction or histories of scientific discovery, these topics can also be found in poetry. Observation and exploration shape Diane Ackerman's *Jaguar of Sweet Laughter* (1993), with its comets, radar, hummingbirds, and verse dedicated to Carl Sagan. Nor are science and technology simply a feature of contemporary verse, as scholarly work establishing Emily Dickinson's knowledge of plants or the Victorian author Leslie Stephen's familiarity with alpine hiking reveal. Each genre, and each era, reflects on the ways science forces a sort of social and personal reckoning with its assumptions and possibilities. Multiple works by A. R. Ammons also demonstrate the potentials for such cross-pollination and complex reverie—his first collection, *Ommateum* (1955), takes its title from the compound eye of an insect.

It is true that science writing was long assumed to have a particular tone, a way of rendering language impenetrably dense and virtually meaningless to nonspecialists. That voice is often parodied, as in Douglas Adams's *Hitchhiker's Guide to the Galaxy* (1979). The book opens with language that swings wildly between the technical and the colloquial, cloaking implicit judgments in a welter of detail intended to signal the speaker's superior knowledge and perspective:

> Far out in the uncharted backwaters of the unfashionable end of the Western Spiral arm of the Galaxy lies a small unregarded yellow sun. Orbiting this at a distance of roughly ninety-eight million miles is an utterly insignificant little blue-green planet. (3)

Elsewhere, Adams concocts a writer's flailing efforts to make an involved technical, if fictitious, phenomenon comprehensible to ordinary individuals who need only its practical applications:

The Babel fish . . . is small, yellow and leechlike, and probably the oddest thing in the Universe. It feeds on brainwave energy received not from its own carrier but from those around it. It absorbs all unconscious mental frequencies from this brainwave energy to nourish itself with.

The overview of the fish's workings continues in this polysyllabic way, until the entry concludes colloquially: "The practical upshot of this is that if you stick a Babel fish in your ear you can instantly understand anything said to you."[5] We recognize when Adams mimics tendentious scientific writing and when he abandons it to tell us what we need to know, implying that it is the language that is complicated and not the subject itself. Fortunately, we are in an era when some scientists may write with their field's technical jargon for one another, but others have invested time and effort in creating prose that resonates with ordinary readers, providing information to those outside the scientific community.

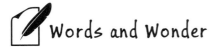# Words and Wonder

Using some of the tools and resources outlined in this chapter, locate a particular scientific word that is genuinely new to you. It can be anything that provokes your imagination and wonder: a plant, a solar system, a disease, and so on. The British naturalist and author Robert Macfarlane, for example, is well-known for his documentation of how specific, distinctive terms arise because of features that are specific to place. *Landmarks* (2016) is one of his critically acclaimed works, the first chapter of which was published in the *Guardian* newspaper as "The Word-Hoard."[6] In your word-search, use multiple sources and media, and give yourself time to gain a sense of how your word fits into larger systems (not just the plumage of the waterthrush, but its migration patterns).

When you're ready to write, make your word the working title of your piece, regardless of the genre you've chosen. Imagine writing back to yourself at the moment when you first encountered this word, and pay attention to how you are introducing it on the page. Remember that the word doesn't have to be the first thing your poem mentions or the first topic your characters are talking about, but it is your poem's title, so you'll probably want to get around to it at some early point. Try to keep the reader from needing or wanting to set your text aside in order to type the term into a search engine. The goal here is not to enact a data dump, but to make this particular term intrigue the reader as much as it intrigued you.

If writers in your community want to create works like Dava Sobel's *Longitude* (1995) or *Galileo's Daughter* (1999); if they are inspired by the life story of Stephen Hawking or Neil deGrasse Tyson; if they thrill to the words of Ursula LeGuin or Ray Bradbury; or if they binge-watch *SciShow* or the Discovery Channel, they are likely to want to draw on these scientific topics and themes in the stories they tell. In the sections below we will give a brief survey of some recent work inflected by these more technical and scientific considerations before offering advice about resources and search strategies for finding information to support this type of writing. Some consideration of the role of observation, the basis for empirical research, is also important to thinking about science-based writing.

CONTEMPORARY SCIENCE WRITING

Librarians looking for science-based writing, whether to create displays or to support programming, have plenty of contemporary titles to draw on. Books that address long-standing problems, like disease and mortality, continue to see publication, while newer topics, like women in science, are gaining in number. Whether you want to familiarize yourself with this type of work or simply intend to suggest models for the writers in your community, several recognized authors have produced distinctive, authoritative nonfiction and fiction that explore the fields of science, technology, and medicine.

Richard Selzer, who died in 2016, is one of a number of noted contemporary writers who are also credentialed scientific practitioners. Selzer was trained as a surgeon but turned to writing stories when he felt his "dexterity was decreasing."[7] His first three books focused on the profession he felt compelled to quit.

The neurologist Oliver Sacks, also recently deceased, is much appreciated in some quarters, while other critics complain that his clinical practice seems to have served his writing more than he served his patients.[8] As his website notes, the *New York Times* once called him "the poet laureate of medicine," and his stature is hard to dispel. His early work, in particular, examines the way that neurological ailments afflict the mind and body alike. Titles like *Migraine,* first published in 1970, exemplify this earlier work. If you are interested in directing writers to something other than text, Sacks's website includes a section called "Inspired by Sacks" that lists movies and documentaries based on his life and work.

Lewis Thomas is best known for *Lives of a Cell* (1974), and most of his books are STEM-focused. Similarly, Stephen Jay Gould, who wrote fairly imposing, more extended books on evolution and paleontology, also published shorter, more accessible works. He had a column in *Natural History* magazine for decades and crafted pieces for the *New York Review of Books,* which were collected into their own volumes every few years. He has a dazzling and engaging style and wrote about bridging the sciences and humanities in *The Hedgehog, the Fox and the Magister's Pox* (2003).

More recent and diverse examples include Abraham Verghese, who is best known for his novel *Cutting for Stone* (2009), but he also wrote nonfiction, particularly a book called *My Own Country* (1994) about his work with AIDS patients. Rafael Campo is another doctor who writes about working with this community. Primarily a poet, he has also published a nonfiction book called *The Desire to Heal* (1998). Nawal El Saadawi is a physician, psychiatrist, and surgeon, in addition to being a writer and human rights advocate. She is now best known for *The Hidden Face of Eve* (1980), but her first novel, *Memoirs of a Woman Doctor* (1988), has also been translated from Arabic into English. Some content, though, has been excised, and therefore lost, by Egyptian censors.[9]

Writers and readers alike are seeking out stories of women in science. Recent titles of interest include Hope Jahren's *Lab Girl*

(2016), winner of the National Book Critics Circle award for autobiography; and Dava Sobel's *Glass Universe: How the Ladies of the Harvard Observatory Took the Measure of the Stars* (2016), which also won critical notice. Kate Moore's *The Radium Girls* (2017) and Denise Kerman's *The Girls of Atomic City: The Untold Story of the Women Who Helped Win World War II* (2013) are also among the newer books that focus on women's critical involvement in major scientific events. In addition to narratives that uncover women's participation in discoveries long attributed to their male colleagues, there are books that explore women's stories in now-conventional professional roles, like nursing. As a *New York Times* review of Christie Watson's *The Language of Kindness: A Nurse's Story* observes, "Many doctors have been distinguished writers. . . . But we haven't heard enough from nurses, whose world is just as arcane and important."[10]

Braiding Sweetgrass: Indigenous Wisdom, Scientific Knowledge, and the *Teachings of Plants* (2013) is a book that traces the connections between tradition and science. Written by Robin Wall Kimmerer, a Native American botanist and distinguished professor at the State University of New York, this is a much-praised work that evaluates the intersections between professionally constructed knowledge of natural phenomena and cultural values and concepts handed down through generations of Potawotami. Boaventura de Sousa Santos is another noteworthy thinker in this area who has written and edited multiple works that complicate and contest received perspectives on science in relation to issues such as biodiversity and social inequality. Particularly of note is his editorial work for the collection *Another Knowledge Is Possible: Beyond Northern Epistemologies* (2009).

Podcasts, too, take on the processes of discovery and learning about the world. Among them is Stephen Fry's delightful *Great Leap Years,* a fast-paced survey of technological developments across history. With more than 500,000 podcasts being produced and released via Apple's platform alone, Fry's work is the tip of the proverbial iceberg, and many lists guide writers to the more exemplary listens.[11]

RECOMMENDATIONS FOR FINDING WELL-WRITTEN SCIENCE

- Tiffany Kelly, "The Eleven Best Science Fiction Novels from the 21st Century You Likely Missed," *Popular Mechanics* (March 22, 2017), https://www.popularmechanics.com/ culture/a25778/best-science-fiction-novels -21st-century/

- *Best Scientific and Technical Writing* annual

- *The Best American Science and Nature Writing* annual

- *Smithsonian* magazine's "Books" section (https://www.smithsonian mag.com/arts-culture/books/)

- NLM Digital Projects (https://www.nlm.nih.gov/digitalprojects.html)

- BBC Computer Literacy Project Archive (https://computer-literacy -project.pilots.bbcconnectedstudio.co.uk/)

RESEARCH STRATEGIES FOR TECHNICAL CONTENT

Research needs and resources for scientific experts differ from those of writers who want scientific details to support their stories. In fact, it is quite likely that writers whose expertise lies outside the sciences will need help finding material that gives them access to the more specialized knowledge and vocabulary of scientists, doctors, and other technical experts. Numerous tools meet this kind of need, but not every public library will possess them. The good news, however, is that federally funded information makes some materials available without subscriptions to costly databases.

There are two major resources produced by the federal government that give researchers access to health information. One, Medline Plus (https://medlineplus.gov/), gathers consumer or non-specialized health information, while the other, PubMed (https://www.ncbi .nlm.nih.gov/pubmed/), indexes medical research. While Medline Plus provides encyclopedia-style overviews of more than 1,000 health-related topics, many of its entries link to further information resources. These resources may be listings of medical trials, emerging research, and patient-oriented newsletters. Because many of its resources are translated into additional languages, primarily Spanish, it offers broad usability. By contrast, the contents of PubMed are often technical, and the most effective searches in it tend to be based on established subject terms listed in MeSH, the index of Medical Subject Headings. While newer federal laws have improved access to research, PubMed is not a full-text database, and even articles that will become public may be embargoed for some months after their release.

While we might expect technical information-seeking to result in hefty reads and linguistically dense articles, YouTube can rescue nonspecialists who seek broad, factual explanations rather than every nuance of a technical scientific problem. YouTube is "the second most popular search engine" and features nearly 400 "popular science, engineering, and mathematics themed channels."[12] Short, authoritative videos from SciShow, Best of Science, Science TV, and other outlets provide information on technical topics, whether contemporary research questions to the history of computing.

Historical perspectives on the intersections between science and health, between biology and the broader subject areas that inform it, tend to be housed in special libraries with good online visibility. First, in the United States, the National Library of Medicine's historical division (https://www.nlm.nih.gov/hmd/) collects older medical materials, including research papers and oral histories of medical practitioners. While some institutions digitize selectively, seeing online material primarily as a way to guide researchers to their physical holdings, grants have sometimes made it possible to digitize entire collections, like the Papers of Isaac Newton at Cambridge University (https://cudl.lib.cam.ac.uk/collections/newton). Other specialized libraries, among them the University of Iowa's John Martin Rare Books Room in the Hardin Health Sciences Library, provide online catalogs that reveal the nature of science and medical writing and research in earlier eras. Older medical books that pair words with pictures are a distinctive phenomenon, and can range from attractively illustrated herbals, which depict and discuss the plants used to formulate medical treatments, to anatomical atlases intended to aid diagnosis in eras before internal imaging was possible. For those unfamiliar with these older books, a word of caution: many are written in Latin. Moreover, most scientific fields originated in the efforts of a relatively small number of men who had the time, money, and educational background to devote themselves to scientific studies, but many institutions now work to document and preserve materials that reflect the ways that race, class, and gender intersected with these fields' development.

Even if your writers are adults, the children's section of your library contains materials that make science and technology comprehensible. Increasingly, children's books on science bring together high-quality information and illustration to spark our curiosity and

BUILDING AND BUILDINGS

More than one writer has bemoaned her less than successful efforts to describe a house, aspiring to better render the sense of place, per her editor's suggestion. Writers quickly recognize that adding more words doesn't necessarily create a better, more vivid picture. Yet, as Matthew Rice reminds us in *Rice's Architectural Primer*, "architecture is all around. It is the backdrop of our lives" (6). Buildings, old or new, are feats of engineering and labor that also reflect the time of their construction. Two particular titles may aid writers who want to know more about the parts of buildings, especially the styles and features associated with different eras and places:

Rice's Architectural Primer (Bloomsbury, 2009). To call this book a text is a misnomer, since it has short introductions to illustrated pages filled with details of cathedrals, schools, mansions, and more. Key architectural features are labeled, proportions are indicated visually, and the book includes a compilation, with miniature representations, of British buildings noted for particular features and construction styles.

What Style Is It? A Guide to American Architecture (Historic Buildings Survey/National Trust for Historic Preservation, 1983). This slender book has chapters highlighting twenty-two prominent architectural styles and eras in U.S. buildings. Photographs and small renderings depict key features. The book includes a glossary that gives short definitions of construction materials, too.

understanding. For adults who want to refresh their knowledge of the details of science, titles like David Macauley's acclaimed and updated *The Way Things Work* can prove valuable. Tackling technology and the human body, his well-regarded books offer uncompromisingly accurate explanations of the workings of things. Graphic representations are central to his analyses, whether of the human eye or the cell phones we use daily. Macauley's books are perhaps the most prominent example of this type of explanatory work, but he is not the only author who wants young readers to have more than a surface knowledge of science and technology, and his books appeal to readers of all ages.

OBSERVATION

Scientific observation, a trained way of looking at the world and recording what one sees, is fundamental to much scientific and technical work. If someone wants to understand causality or other relationships, his attention must be directed to sometimes subtle changes. The principle of observation is manifest in accounts of scientific and mathematical discoveries that have become a kind of folklore: Antonie von Leeuwenhoek's early microscopes that enabled him to see "animalcules" (i.e., microorganisms); Isaac Newton and the concept of gravity that first occurred to him when he watched an apple falling from a tree; and even the probably legendary story about Archimedes's realization of the relationship between weight and water displacement as a means of measuring mass. Ways of looking at the world generate new information and new details about its workings. Within a field or discipline, sharing the means of making and documenting these observations allows people to share information and discuss its implications.

The Philosophical Transactions of the Royal Society (http://rstl.royal societypublishing.org/) claims status as the first scientific journal. Founded in 1665, its early papers shared members' observations. Its first paper, "An Account of the Improvement of Optick Glasses," captures a specific moment in the history of what could be seen

Describing Discovery

Discoveries are inherently dramatic, and every genre of writing manages them in different ways. A discovery might take the form of a concentrated, concluding epiphany that anchors many short stories and poems, though individual discoveries can also push a story from one point to the next, as in most mysteries and plot-driven fiction. This prompt will require you to look into the history of a particular scientific discovery that holds your interest.

In illuminating a moment of scientific discovery, writers should attend to the wider dimensions around the "Eureka!" moment. A writer interested in Marie Curie might consider the theories or mystifications around radioactivity that her discovery displaced. The intent here is to gain access, through research and some imagination, to perspectives that might be regarded as more peripheral to the source of the discovery. Maybe the story precedes Curie's discovery by decades and will include her sister Bronislawa, with whom she took courses at the Flying University in Warsaw, a clandestine organization where women could gain access to higher education. In any case, the weight of a discovery can be relied upon to do a great deal of narrative work, even if it happens offstage. What sort of story would you try to write about the person who emptied Edward Lorenz's office trash in the years following or preceding his description of the butterfly effect?

and thought about scientifically: "It hath been found by experience, that small glasses are in proportion better to see with, upon the Earth, than great ones; that Author affirms that his are equally good for Earth, and for making Observations in the Heavens." From this moment on, with or without lenses, observation and measurement have figured in scientific discoveries.

The findings of Charles Darwin, notably his theory of evolution, are entwined with observation. Darwin scrutinized everything, it seems, and was an inveterate note-taker, harvesting his journals sometimes decades later to construct a coherent theory. Among his lesser-known works, for example, is *The Formation of Vegetable Mould, through the Action of Worms, with Observations on Their Habits* (1882). This treatise studies earthworms, considering everything from the extent of their consciousness to their role in improving soil quality. To produce this work, Darwin observed what was at hand: "I was led to keep in my study during many months worms in pots filled with earth." He also observed what was farther away, like Stonehenge, providing details and figures indicating the stones' positions. Some one hundred pages after his initial start with worms in pots and journeys to English sites, he concludes that "sufficient evidence has now been given showing that small objects left on the surface of the land where worms abound soon get buried, and that large stones sink slowly downward through the same means."[13] He also observed, indirectly, what was not at hand for him to witness directly. He corresponded with other scientists, asking them questions about the conditions where they lived and worked, and he sought out his subject matter in the research literature of the time. For him and for other scientists, observation was a multifaceted endeavor.

Not all of Darwin's writings are so dispassionate. Reading the papers that Darwin generated during his long life reveals their human and sometimes touching details, suggesting why biographers find him so interesting. His children appear in his work, often unexpectedly. His discourse on worms, for example, includes an experiment intended to understand how rapidly worms might change the land. Describing a piece of ground's starting condition, Darwin recalls that "for several years it was clothed with an extremely scant vegetation, and was so thickly covered with small

SCIENCE AS A STORY

- *Darwin's Origin of Species: A Biography* (Grove, 2008), by Janet Browne
- *The Invention of Nature* (Penguin Random House, 2015), by Andrea Wulf
- *Kepler* (Godine, 1983), by John Banville
- *Steve Jobs* (Simon & Schuster, 2011), by Walter Isaacson
- *We Could Not Fail: The First African-Americans in the Space Program* (University of Texas Press, 2015), by Richard Paul and Stephen Moss

and large flints (some of them half as large as a child's head) that the field was always called by my sons 'the stony field.'"[14] His measurements relative to small children remind us that science was never a purely neutral work where its practitioners distanced themselves from what they studied.

 ## Perspectives on Process

Whatever sort of science interests the writers in your community, it certainly has a terminology that reflects the techniques and the significance of observation. Whether scientists measure degrees, time, or other empirical data, they rely on shared norms of observation and recording. With perhaps somewhat different motivations, writers are also invested in observation. Wallace Stevens's "Thirteen Ways of Looking at a Blackbird" is a frequently considered specimen of this sort, with the accompanying exercise of directing writers to generate their own multiple observations of an object and render it in verse. While this is an older exercise, it is worth repeating, especially given that it may not require a great deal of preparation for successful use.

If the library has a makerspace, this too may offer a means of enabling writers to experience the process of discovery, by observing the making process at firsthand. By taking notes as they build, keeping track of their failures, and identifying the features that enable successful project completion, the makerspace serves as a laboratory for writers' discovery processes.

WIDENING THE NET

Science and technology may serve as inspiration or anchor for writers, but those who work with these topics must remember that the elements of writing well in any genre still hold. Strong narrative arc and clear and convincing wording are no less essential for writers who create medical dramas or science fiction than for any other genre. Works with wide-ranging styles and attitudes signal the ways that writers can include more technical content in whatever stories they tell, providing models, inspiration, and a community of kindred practitioners.

This chapter has focused on a few distinctive areas of research and writing. To include or even mention all scientific and technical subjects is beyond its scope. In closing, then, it is worth remembering that if measurement is involved at some stage of discovery or production, there is in all likelihood an organization or a group of researchers who have established norms in the field. A subject search in a database like Organizations Unlimited may serve as a starting point. From old-fashioned wooden watercraft (see *Wooden Boat Magazine,* for starters) to airplanes (see *Jane's All the World's Aircraft*), to the science of steel structures like the Bird's Nest stadium constructed for the 2008 Olympics (see National Geographic's documentary at www.nationalgeographic.com.au/tv/beijing-olympic -stadium/), numerous phenomena reflect both scientific discovery and the application of these findings. Writers, too, can apply these principles in their work.

Notes

1. "Data Tools: Daily Weather Records," National Oceanic and Atmospheric Administration, https://www.ncdc.noaa.gov/cdo-web/datatools/records; "The View of the Frost Fair," Online Gallery, British Library, www.bl.uk/onlinegallery/onlineex/kinggeorge/t/003ktop00000027u04100001.html.

2. "What Are Clinical Trials?" National Cancer Institute (June 27, 2016), https://www.cancer.gov/about-cancer/treatment/clinical-trials/what-are-trials.

3. Anthony Doerr, *All the Light We Cannot See* (New York: Scribner, 2014), 3.

4. Josh Trapani, "Review of *Astrophysics for People in a Hurry,*" *Washington Independent: Review of Books* (May 12, 2017), www.washingtonindependentreviewofbooks.com/index.php/bookreview/astrophysics-for-people-in-a-hurry.

5. Douglas Adams, *The Hitchhiker's Guide to the Galaxy,* 53.

6. Robert Macfarlane, "The Word-Hoard," *The Guardian* (February 27, 2015), https://www.theguardian.com/books/2015/feb/27/robert-macfarlane-word -hoard-rewilding-landscape.

7. Quoted in Randi Hutter Epstein, "Richard Selzer, Who Fictionalized Medicine's Absurdity and Gore, Dies at 87," *New York Times* (June 15, 2016), https://www.nytimes.com/2016/06/16/books/richard-selzer-who-fictional ized-medicines-absurdity-and-gore-dies-at-87.html. See also Richard Selzer, excerpt from *The Surgeon as Priest, The Sun* (January 2016), https://www .thesunmagazine.org/issues/481/the-surgeon-as-priest.

8. Adam Zeman, "Oliver Sacks: Obituary," *The Guardian* (August 30, 2015), https://www.theguardian.com/books/2015/aug/30/oliver-sacks.

9. Dora Carpenter-Latiri, "The Reading Room: A Review of 'Memoirs of a Woman Doctor,'" *Medical Humanities* blog (November 11, 2015), https://blogs .bmj.com/medical-humanities/2015/11/11/the-reading-room-a-review-of -memoirs-of-a-woman-doctor/.

10. Roxana Robinson, "Christie Watson Is a Lovely Writer—and, Judging from This Book, a Gifted Nurse," *New York Times* (June 27, 2018), https:// www.nytimes.com/2018/06/27/books/review/christie-watson-language -kindness.html.

11. "The 20 Best Science Podcasts," GeekWrapped (n.d.), https://www.geek wrapped.com/posts/the-20-best-science-podcasts.

12. Inoka Amarasekara and Will J. Grant, "Exploring the YouTube Science Communication Gender Gap: A Sentiment Analysis," *Public Understanding of Science* (July 5, 2018), https://doi.org/10.1177/0963662518786654.

13. Charles Darwin, *The Formation of Vegetable Mould, through the Action of Worms, with Observations on Their Habits* (British Library General Historical Collection, reprint of London, 1882), 2, 159.

14. Ibid., 145.

7

Place and Space

et's say that *place* is simply what you can say about where you find yourself right now. Maybe it includes the feeling of this book in your hands, the chair you're sitting on, the temperature making you sweat or shiver, or the sounds at the edge of your attention. The most immediate points of sensory contact that you have with the world will inform your sense of the particular place that surrounds you. *Space,* by contrast, is more open and abstract: Rio de Janeiro. A half-built bridge in a black-and-white photograph. The rings of Saturn. An echoing concrete stairwell. The ocean. While these locations might not have much to do with the place where you actually are, they name or evoke spaces that, regardless of where you're reading, create a sort of portal from where you're sitting to somewhere else. This sense that the right words transport us is an enduring one. We see it in Emily Dickinson's declaration that there is "no frigate like a book / to take us worlds away," and it even echoes in the title theme to the educational TV show *Reading Rainbow,* whose singer has an open ticket to "go anywhere" because of books.

This influential distinction between space and place is indebted to the geographer Yi-Fu Tuan, who holds that while place "is security, space is freedom: we are attached to the one and long for the other."[1] That libraries serve as a place of refuge is not news to those who work in them and use them, though we are also accustomed to thinking of them as sites of freedom. One useful critique of Tuan's paradigm comes from Doreen Massey, who has pointed out how readily the distinction between place and space reinforces gender binaries: place is synonymous with home and hearth, fixity and femininity, while space is, predictably, for exploration and conquering, a proving ground for men. We would be better served, Massey contends, by paying more attention to the ways in which any given place proves to be "unfixed, contested and multiple" once we begin to engage it.[2] These characterizations of space and place play into the immediate opportunities and challenges present within libraries and learning spaces.

To put it another way, place, as Rebecca Solnit has written,

> is the intersection of many changing forces passing through, whirling around, mixing, dissolving, and exploding in a fixed location. To write about a place is to acknowledge that phenomena often treated separately—ecology, democracy, culture, storytelling, urban design, individual life histories and collective endeavors—coexist.[3]

This is one reason not to maintain a strict space/place distinction, though another is more obvious: these terms are used interchangeably by most of us. Accordingly, this chapter defers to this wider, practical fact of common usage.

This chapter provides a combination of readings and prompts that pivot on questions of space and place as they present themselves in any creative work: through elements like framing, tone, abstraction, pacing, and point of view. Maintaining this focus means paying more attention to how a writer enables a reader's attention to move, question, and conceptualize the contours of a spatial world rendered into language.

LADDERS AND THRESHOLDS

The landscape of Moshim Hamid's novel *Exit West* (2017) changes when rumors begin to circulate of doors that could take you elsewhere, often away, well removed from this death trap of a country. Some people claimed to know people who had been through such doors. A normal door, they said, could become a special door, and it could happen without warning, to any door at all. Most people thought these rumors to be nonsense, the superstitions of the feeble-minded. But most people began to gaze at their own doors a little differently nonetheless.[4]

When the doors prove to be more than a rumor, no further explanation of their power is given that might reconcile them with received reality, but in a novel examining the human consequences of civil war, Hamid's supernatural flourishes are not fanciful. They draw the narration closer to that of a fable, even as it feels suffused with the headlines of 2017, its publication year, in large part because the reader is never told the name of "this death trap of a country." This vagueness is purposeful, and it depends on what is called the "ladder of abstraction."[5] This ladder can be applied to any piece of description: a *car* can be a *vehicle,* a *machine,* or just an *object.* It can also be a *Volkswagen* or a *1978 VW Beetle Convertible.* Writers move up and down the ladder as needed, when describing spaces as well as objects, sometimes intuitively and sometimes with more deliberation.

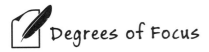 Degrees of Focus

Try introducing the passage from Hamid's book alongside one or two other examples of your choosing, looking for what will best convey the possibilities inherent in both a vivid specificity and a more smudged, generalized outline. For example, an early chapter of Qiu Miaojin's novel *Notes of a Crocodile* (2017) pinpoints the narrator's first sight of her beloved: "Shui Ling. Wenzhou Street. The white bench in front of the French bakery. The number 74 bus . . . The December fog is sealed off behind glass. Dusk starts to set in around six, enshrouding Taipei" (9). In contrast, Zadie Smith's third-person narration in *NW* (2012) will pass through three vibrant sentences before turning to her central character: "The fat sun stalls by the phone masts. Anti-climb paint turns sulphurous on school gates and lampposts. In Willesden people go barefoot, the streets turn European, there is a mania for eating outside. She keeps to the shade. Redheaded" (3).

The power of Hamid's withholding the name of the country in which his narrative begins might be amplified by pairing it with one of Franz Kafka's short parables, such as "Before the Law." In any case, you can create a context in which patrons can talk about word choice and its consequences in more than one of the examples for up to ten minutes. At this point, have the group disperse and encourage everyone to find a spot within or near the library where they can write a sustained description of what's around them. Upon reconvening, have patrons experiment with changing some of the crucial words in their sentences and notes using the ladder of abstraction, before sharing their results.

One possible takeaway assignment would be to encourage patrons to follow the same method with a memory. Another would be to ask participants to re-describe the same space after it has been transformed in some way: by the loss or addition of particular people, or simply by changes in the weather; after a restoration or a long period of negligence; or as the setting for a holiday gathering or street festival. What direction is this place heading in? Where is the story? What are the most striking images? What happens next?

Henry David Thoreau's "Walking" might be the most famous example of the ambulatory essay, but walking can also hold together entire books—Cheryl Strayed's *Wild* (2016), Rebecca Solnit's *Wanderlust* (2001), and W. G. Sebald's incomparable *The Rings of Saturn* (1998), among others. Walking does not lend itself to any set style or format. The impressions that Virginia Woolf gathers together in her essay "Street Haunting" have been folded into a dreamy, urgent rhythm:

> How beautiful a street is in winter! It is at once revealed and obscured. Here vaguely one can trace symmetrical straight avenues of doors and windows; here under the lamps are floating islands of pale light through which pass quickly bright men and women, who, for all their poverty and shabbiness, wear a certain look of unreality, an air of triumph, as if they had given life the slip, so that life, deceived by

her prey, blunders on without them. But, after all, we are only glid-
ing smoothly on the surface. The eye is not a miner, not a diver, not
a seeker after buried treasure. It floats us smoothly down a stream;
resting, pausing, the brain sleeps perhaps as it looks.[6]

Woolf's prose allows us to experience space as a recursive construction, with emerging and dissolving sense impressions shifting into
general observations that provide a commentary on perception itself.

A little less than ninety years later in Manhattan, we can see an
approach that allows the writing to become (or remain) more circum-
stantial and fragmented in the work of the poet Stacy Szymaszek,
who plays incongruous, vivid snippets against one another, with
backslashes serving as the textual equivalent of cinematic jump-
cuts: "East Village: cartoon M&M's key chain hanging from ATM
sign // plastic waste from 9 people devouring take-out sushi // it's a
mural of a purple tree with a long green nose and eyeballs // hoard
of women at 16 Handles // choir singing national anthem panicking
getting out so fast zip drive somehow slipping out of silky pockets GONE despite searching through cobblestones."[7] Each of these
writers has found a way to let their walking lead them into a style
and flexibility of thought that feels inextricable from the promise of
the freedom to move.

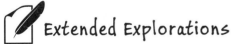

Extended Explorations

While it may not always be clear where a piece of writing or its author ultimately want to go, there are different ways of picturing and sustaining an
ongoing curiosity about what remains just beyond one's location or gaze. The
National Book Award-winning poet Nathaniel Mackey recently described his
early practices as a reader:

> The experience of reading, for me, was an experience of enlargement.
> I used to do this thing when I was a teenager; every night I would fig-
> ure out the farthest point west I had been, the farthest point north, the
> farthest point east and the farthest point south that day. And I would
> compare the compass of my physical movement with the compass of

my mental movement through reading . . . that sense of enlargement was very clear to me . . . in the sense of touching some other person's experience, so that it's a way of moving and a way of being moved . . . I would like that to be what my writing offers to readers.[8]

Simply trying to imitate Mackey's habit would be a useful way to raise our awareness of the patterns and limits present in these daily excursions; however, if writers are looking for more structure, they may want to try keeping a log of their locations and related readings. A process like this can also be combined with more formalized ways of intertwining the act of walking (patrons with mobility issues can adapt this prompt to their modalities) with the act of writing.

First, writers should take a notebook, a timepiece, and a pen or pencil with them to a place they are curious about. This place can be familiar or unfamiliar, but in general writers will be better off choosing a spot where they are less likely to run into friends. It is crucial not to send or receive calls or texts for the duration of the exercise, so writers who normally use cell phones to keep time should choose another method.

Now divide a piece of notebook paper into five columns. Label them *vision, hearing, touch, smell,* and *taste.* Details and observations should each be written into the relevant column and all of them should be used. The goal of this exercise is not to put entire lines or sentences into these columns. Instead, writers should focus on individual words and phrases.

The exercise itself requires about an hour to complete and has three parts which can be done in any order. Every twenty minutes will be given over to trying out different ways of relating writing, walking, and observation to one another. They run as follows:

1. Walk at a relaxed pace with your notebook open, writing down your observations. Slow down as needed in order to maintain legible handwriting, but try to stay more or less on the move for the full twenty minutes.

2. Remain sitting or standing in a particular spot where it is possible to see in multiple directions comfortably. Write as much as possible.

3. Put away the notebook and walk. Pay attention. When twenty minutes have passed, sit down and write out everything seen, smelled, heard, touched, and tasted, with as much detail as possible.

Writers should wait a few days before returning to look over what they've written in order to think about what these different methods offered, how they were challenging (or not), and which of them fit with the writer's sensibilities. This is an exercise that gets more interesting with repetition and can be used to highlight many questions that recur for any writer. How does speed or slowness get conveyed on the page? How and when does the act of writing change our ordinary ways of perceiving? What do we miss by choosing not to stay still? How do we decide what's interesting? Amidst the din of activities and data surrounding us, how will we track down what Chekhov termed the "telling detail"?

Another significant facet of this exercise is that it allows for time to reframe one's notes, whether they are individual sentences or poetic lines, into something else. Writers might find themselves remembering additional details after rereading those they copied down, or realize how distracted they had been by something during the walk and how they can now, by writing about it, accompany and complicate what is already on the page.

SIZE AND SCALE, FIGURE AND GROUND

Writers continually grapple with the challenge of how to represent what is enormous, whether it is a mountain or a planet, and exceedingly miniscule objects—cells, motes, particles, and atoms— present a similar difficulty. Because every kind of magnitude remains relative, it is almost always in reference to the human body that a work of prose or poetry begins to render the world, or some part of it, for its reader. Hannah Arendt argues that metrics actually conceal crucial aspects of how we understand size and distance, maintaining that once we render nature into numbers, we both domesticate it and make it less real: "Only the wisdom of hindsight sees the obvious: that nothing can remain immense if it can be measured. Thus, the maps and navigation charts of the early stages of the modern age anticipated the technical inventions through which all earthly space has become small . . . Before we knew how to circumscribe the sphere of human habitation in days and hours, we had brought the globe into our living rooms to be touched by our hands and swirled before our eyes."[9] Arendt is describing the transformation of European consciousness through trade and imperialism, but if we step away from her historical argument to consider her contention about measurement, it may be difficult to agree unequivocally with her. Whether a passing notation of the Milky Way's 100,000 estimated light years makes it *feel* immensely encompassing or immensely removed from the reader is hard for the writer to know. Metrics may have only limited means of conveying qualities of vastness or emptiness as they relate to space without falling into stupefaction and redundancy. Something else usually needs to happen, and here the skillful use of words enters the picture. In the following examples, the trick depends on scale and rhythm.

Consider Rachel Carson's meditation in *The Sea Around Us:*

> Every part of the earth or air or sea has an atmosphere peculiarly its own, a quality or characteristic that sets it apart from all others. When I think of the floor of the deep sea, the single, overwhelming fact that possesses my imagination is the accumulation of sediments. I see always the steady, unremitting, downward drift of materials from above, flake upon flake, layer upon layer—a drift that has continued for hundreds of millions of years, that will go on as long as there are seas and continents.[10]

Here a vast space and immense periods of time are rendered through the author's focus on individual flakes of sediment as they settle onto the seafloor. This is the distinction between size and scale that bears repeating: size might be conveyed by adjectives or by a recorded weight, height, and so on. Scale, though, expresses the relations between things, a measurement of one object against another. In this spirit, compare Carson's drifting sediment to the churn of snowflakes that begins Larry Levis's poem:

> The snow that has no name is just
> This snow, falling so thick it seems
> To pause a moment in midair.
> When I had stared long enough at it, the word
> That held it showed me only a swirling without
> A name, a piece of untalkative sky intact

Above a row of houses, & blankness filling
The frames of every doorway, a white
That made the dark around it visible.[11]

Both of these passages create a sense of enormity through their attention to small but serene moments of animated suspension. These achievements are arrived at through sound (repeated words, alliteration, and assonance) and extension (Carson's second sentence almost triples the length of her first), rather than by any straightforward conceptual illustration.

As space becomes more charged with contrasts, the tone, mood, or affect that emanates from it also becomes more complicated and nuanced. The shifting tension between the past and present tense is crucial to both preceding passages as they attempt to focus and trace an ongoing, escaping *now*. Another kind of interplay between the past and present is on display in the opening moves of two short stories from contemporary masters of the form as they bring us into the particular places from which we'll begin. Both authors use distinct approaches to characterizing place, introducing the reader to a particular point in the world that feels tangibly real.

Here is Alice Munro:

It was called, even that summer, my grandma's house, though my grandfather was then still alive. He had withdrawn into one room, the largest front bedroom. It had wooden shutters on the inside of the windows, like the living room and dining room; the other bedrooms had only blinds. Also, the veranda kept out the light so that my grandfather lay in near-darkness all day, with his white hair, now washed and tended and soft as a baby's, and his white nightshirt and pillows, making an island in the room which people approached with diffidence, but resolutely.[12]

And here is Christine Schutt:

Used to be even in the rain we walked hooded in water-repellent bicolor suits that swished and sounded as if we were fat when we were thin, both of us, Margaret and I, and only walking for the routine and way it felt, hands free, holding nothing. Children, leashes—my first husband—we left the dogs sleeping to meet each other at the entrance to the park marked by the great elm, the folktale tree with its house-wide trunk sprung green. We meet there still although not as often—and no more in the rain.[13]

Each of these passages contorts time slightly as the past is placed vividly in front of the reader, almost as if it were the present, with individuals conjured even as their absence is marked. As we attend to each writer's handling of place, we notice the contrast that Munro has rendered between the darkness of the room and the little island of white constituted by the grandfather's nightshirt, pillows, and baby-soft hair; the latter have a haunting luminosity that feels both gentle and imposing. We feel somewhat shy to be looking into this room. Schutt's narrator begins wistfully in the past, then puts the reader at an intersectional space where we meet her friend, whose cancer we will soon learn about. She stands beside the broad trunk of an elm which is itself a kind of intersection, one where this mortal world meets one of folk tales. The trunk's width makes her thinness thinner.

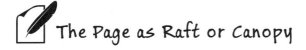 The Page as Raft or Canopy

With reference to some or all of the passages above, writing group leaders can craft a specific prompt that encourages participants to write about different kinds of spatial relationships, contrasts, and extremes. In addition to the examples provided above, the fantastical spaces described in classic works like Jonathan Swift's *Gulliver's Travels* or Jorge Luis Borges's "The Library of Babel" could be useful models for the creation of individual scenes and fictional worlds.

Ask participants what sorts of strategies they find most useful for describing the enormous and the miniscule. How would they describe the very near or the very distant? How does each of these challenges involve tone, mood, and affect? What do we mean when we say that something in a piece of writing *feels* distant? Or that it is pressing down on us?

Alternatively, you can encourage writers to begin with a particular place they associate with a distinct feeling (comfort, trepidation, wonderment, boredom, etc.) and give them time to elaborate a description of that spot. Then ask for another description of another place, one that changed forever, in their eyes, when a single event occurred. With these examples in front of them, encourage them to consider which of the prompts produced more interesting material.

LIMITED FAMILIARITY

Evaluating when to use a word or phrase that many readers might be unfamiliar with is a perennial question for any writer, since it comes back to the possibilities and risks inherent in vocabulary itself. There is no absolute answer to this question. It is not difficult to stop and consult a dictionary before returning to any piece of writing, even if this also breaks the narrative spell. The more important consideration is simply this: what kind of work is a comparatively unfamiliar word, name, or phrase doing in the context of your description?

We are standing with Neal Ascherson at the outset of his essay:

> Here is the forest. Not just a forest, but a *puszcza*: a Polish word that means a world of trees which have never been felled since the first bands of human beings arrived to hunt here. The *Puszcza* of Kniszyn, which begins north-east of the Polish city of Bialystok, must be 10,000 years old.

> To reach the village of Lipowy Most, I set off from the city Bialystok along the road which leads to the Soviet frontier. I turned off the tarred highway at the spot where an oak tree grows upon a mound, a tree on which the Russians hanged Polish insurgents during the January Rising of 1863. That is to say: the vain Polish insurrection for independence which began in January but which lasted for fifteen months—for even longer, in the *puszcza*.[14]

It is hard to imagine a sentence more simple and direct than the one Ascherson begins with, but as we quickly discover, it is the ghosts that define this forest, where human time is marked by violence, which has been absorbed with an eerie equanimity by towering trees. This is why the forest is not just a forest, but a *puszcza*.

Sometimes the ground disappears beneath us as we try to figure out if a particular detail is obscuring or revealing what we want the reader to experience. *Puszca* anchors the space in something that is both specific and historical, but still very much estranged from the English-speaking reader. In this instance, a foreign word does something that the recitation of facts simply cannot do. Librarians seeking a poem that sharpens and complicates some of these claims, while approaching them within a different form and setting, might pair Eavan Boland's poem "That the Science of Cartography Is Limited" with the passage by Ascherson.[15]

Toni Morrison was asked to describe the kind of research she did to create her novel *A Mercy* (2008), which is set in the early colonial United States. She explained that while attempting to put this world on the page posed real challenges,

> I had a lot of help because historians and anthropologists and biologists have been writing about the era for years. The first thing I had to do was find out what was there—the plant life, the tree life, the weather. One book that was most helpful, which I read over and over, was *Changes in the Land* by William Cronon. I could find out if there really was lettuce or dandelions or how big the trees were. So that gave me a grounded sense of the places that I had chosen, which were upstate New York and down in Maryland and Virginia.[16]

Thinking about how books get inside of one another is another useful challenge for conceptualizing space as it is written (and rewritten) across different genres and times. Each of these authors is intensely interested in how Europeans were processing their surroundings, but they proceed differently when evoking settlers' experience of what was in front of them, both known and unknown. Here is Cronon: "For the entirety of the sixteenth century, maps of New England consisted of a single line separating ocean from land, accompanied by a string of place-names to indicate landmarks along the shore; the interior remained blank."[17]

And here is Morrison:

> The man moved through the surf, stepping carefully over pebbles and sand to shore. Fog, Atlantic and reeking of plant life, blanketed

the bay and slowed him . . . Unlike the English fogs he had known since he could walk, or those way north where he lived now, this one was sun fired, turning the world into thick, hot gold. Penetrating it was like struggling through a dream.[18]

In each of these passages, we have a combination of images to work with: a shoreline followed by a string of place-names; and a fog that is like walking into a blank space, suffused with the promise and menace of gold and fire.

If, as the novelist Tommy Orange observed in a recent interview, "the land is everywhere and nowhere," Cronon and Morrison illustrate distinct ways of capturing that sensation, wherein what is at hand and what is unknown overlap. Orange, discussing his work as a Native American author, continues with words that echo those written by James Baldwin more than fifty years earlier: "you can read . . . an intimate detail that a writer writes about, and you have this feeling, like, oh, my God, I didn't know anybody else thought like that or did that."[19] Attaching a resonant image to a sensation, whether it informs the reader of an unreachable or disappeared space, or about one hidden in plain sight, demonstrates how we inhabit the world. While writing is always a part of how any territory is fought for, it can also be a conduit for proposing that something is shared between two strangers, aside from their residence on planet Earth.

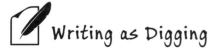 **Writing as Digging**

As a way to begin or extend discussion and generative work around readings like these, librarians might encourage participants to try versions of the following prompt: seek out a place you are provoked by in some way. You don't have to know exactly why. While every place is unique in some way, make a point of finding one that is also reproducible and common: a stoop, a meadow, a bridge, creek, or alleyway. Expect to make multiple visits to this place. Begin with some of the attentive, descriptive writing that has been happening in previous prompts. Take as little or as much time as you need. Then get away from the place and start researching. Try to figure out how to pivot from a very general starting point into a deeper dive into what is particular to *that* stoop or meadow, the one you want to put before the reader's eyes. Are you sitting in a park that was once on the edge of town? What is the history of automatic doors? Is the rhythm they create for the waiting room something you can put into your poem? The goal here is to let the page shape itself to the space, with little, particular facts as the attachments.

Alternatively, if you are hosting a writing group in a library meeting room and prefer to remain there, pull oversize photo books from your holdings and use them as source material to get writers thinking about other spaces. Collections like Annie Leibowitz's *Pilgrimage* or Stephen Shore's *American Surfaces* might be useful, along with work from people like William Eggleston, Gordon Parks, Zoe Leonard, Andreas Gursky, Uta Barth, Santu Mofokeng, or Martin Parr.

INVENTORIES AND PROLIFERATION

Literary uses of the list have a long and broad history, but when thinking about space, place, and their particularities, writers are continually confronted with variations on one question: what objects and features could belong in my description, and why? Any sentence with a noun in it offers some sort of answer, but something quite different happens when a piece of writing suddenly presents the reader with an extended collection of items—whether they arrive in a haphazard flood, follow an obvious pattern, or seem meticulously arranged by their own internal logic. Lists turn up for lots of reasons, and writers should consider them as they seek to record and invent.

Shaping a Pocket

A fairly straightforward exercise can begin by asking participants to make a single inventory of objects—not a story, essay, or poem with an inventory somewhere in it, but an actual list that they feel is as long and detailed as it needs to be. The things on the list can be fictional or factual, something ready at hand (the contents of a pocket) or less so (all the reasons to quit your job). This list can be a starting point for considering some published examples with very different tones and purposes. Two longer, published examples (not reproduced in full below) can be found in Sinclair Lewis's novel *It Can't Happen Here* (1935) and Marilynne Robinson's *Housekeeping* (1980), which should be photocopied and distributed to participants.

In the third chapter of Lewis's novel we are first in the home of his protagonist, Vermont newspaperman Doremus Jessup, and then in his study. This study is

> his one perfect refuge from annoyances and bustle . . . an endearing mess of novels, copies of the *Congressional Record,* of the *New Yorker, Time, Nation, New Republic, New Masses,* and *Speculum* (cloistral organ of the Medieval Society), treatises on taxation and monetary systems . . . chewed stubs of pencils, a shaky portable typewriter, fishing tackle, rumpled carbon paper, two comfortable old leather chairs . . . a fine, reputedly Tudor oak cabinet from Devonshire . . . twenty-four boxes of safety matches one by one stolen from the kitchen.[20]

Amidst the clutter of the nearly 500-word paragraph that describes the room, the objects are telling the story of their owner, but the author is also seeking to carve out a sociological, sardonic outline of his main character through the voice of a fairly distant third-person narrator..

Ruth, the narrator of Robinson's novel, handles things differently as she digs through a drawer in her grandmother's room, finding "balls of twine, Christmas candles, and odd socks . . . contents . . . so randomly assorted, yet so neatly arranged, that we felt some large significance might be behind the collection as a whole." Examining this passage—which extends across multiple pages, concluding with the question: "What are all these fragments for, if not to be knit up finally?"—we see a list take on elements of lyricism, mystery, and ultimately transcendence, which are simply not part of the picture for Doremus. Robinson braids her items with more narration, across multiple paragraphs, but it is the style that creates consequences.[21] Studying these two examples, or others that provide a stark contrast, allows writers to become more conscious of what might be possible for their own lists. Either or both of these examples could be placed next to one of Sei Shonagon's brief, impeccable, and hyper-specific lists from *The Pillow Book* to create a different conversation.

While lists depend on new items continually appearing, the use and pleasure of repetition can also be part of how they unfold. Claire-Louise Bennett's *Pond* (2015) creates an inventory with a swell of near-manic exuberance. While it must be quoted at length for participants to sense the effect, it begins this way:

> There were so many flowers already in bloom when I moved in: wisteria, fuchsia, roses, golden chain, and many other kinds of flowering trees and shrubs I do not know the names of—many of them wild—and all in great abundance . . . I spent most days out the front there, padding and out all day long, and the air was absolutely buzzing with so many different species of bee and wasp, butterfly, dragonfly, and birds, so many birds, and all of them so busy. Everything: every plant, every flower, every bird, every insect, just getting on with it.[22]

Bennett's euphonious prose creates a mood through the music of naming, making a place teem with the movement and churn of every living thing passing in and out of the narrator's awareness. This structured momentum reshapes itself inside that huge, vague word: *Everything*. We experience both the narrator's hyperactivity, her mimicking of every plant and animal "just getting on with it" and then, in the unquoted portion that follows, we see her setting about her real work, which is to extend her sensibility vertically, listening to the stratosphere and then back to the "dusk and earth," returning back inside to attend to her own appetite for chopped walnuts, white cheese, and spinach.

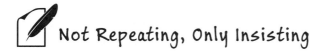 Not Repeating, Only Insisting

With these examples in their ears, writers might try the following: seek out a place with a comfortable hum of activity and try to translate that sound onto the page. Alternatively, go to a bare, quiet place and attempt the same. For an additional challenge, render each of these places with roughly the same number of words. Is it possible to render them in a counterintuitive mode (e.g., the serenely cacophonous interior of a shopping mall) by shifting your style, tone, or diction?

Alternatively, you can pair Bennett's passage with the following one, which emphasizes that repetition can create many kinds of music, including the petulant, comic bleakness that comes near the beginning of Lynda Barry's novel *Cruddy:* "Once upon a cruddy time on a cruddy street on the side of a cruddy hill in the cruddiest part of a crudded-out town in a cruddy state, country, world, solar system, universe. Once upon a cruddy time behind a cruddy Black Cat Lumber on a very cruddy mud road . . . a cruddy girl named Roberta was writing the cruddy book of her cruddy life and the name of the book was called Cruddy."[23]

Calling a piece of writing "repetitive" is sometimes an inadequate description of what's happening on the level of language. Often, what is meant by "repetitive" is that we're bored with the level of continuity in terms of tone, emotion, or event. Things might keep feeling and sounding the same without literally replaying the same bits of language; however, when we engage directly with tools like anaphora (the repetition of the same word at the start of successive phrases or sentences), different textures, contours, and relationships to space may become possible. Writers looking for extended demonstrations of such practices might consult the work of Walt Whitman and Gertrude Stein, whose expansive relationships to writing and space were facilitated enormously by their choices to repeat words and expressions.

With that in mind, the next exercise is simple: describe a place with full permission to repeat single words, phrases, sentences, or single sounds. Try overdoing it, playing with patterns, or making meticulous rules (i.e., a paragraph about home with only one vowel sound allowed).

BARRIERS, EDGES, AND PUNCTURES

Borders are made and enforced by writing, even when walls, rivers, and mountain ranges are present on the ground. But writing can also contest, complicate, and reimagine them. The usefulness of borders for writers is partially bound up with the opportunity they provide for noticing how reality is divided, whether into nation-states, neighborhoods, or informal psychological arenas. Trying to describe the transitions between places requires us to notice how borders unify spaces even as they divide them; this is true whether I am examining the line between my apartment and the hallway, a front yard and a sidewalk, or the food court inside a mall and the bus interchange just outside its doors.

As with the preceding sections of this chapter, this one assumes that first-hand, site-specific investigations into local delineations of space can gain depth in combination with readings in disparate settings. Borders and their consequences are at the core of a wide range of recent literature in various genres, in books such as *The City and the City* by China Miéville (2009), *Midnight's Children* by Salman Rushdie (1981), *Dictee* by Theresa Hak Kyung Cha (1982), *The Devil's Highway* by Luis Alberto Urrea (2008), *Imperial* by William T. Vollmann (2009), and *Brother, I'm Dying* by Edwidge Danticat (2007). The heightened tension of a border crossing also lends itself to short forms, like the lyric poem, which can be read in a sitting. Placing two approaches next to one another—such as Seamus Heaney's "From the Frontier of Writing" and Juan Felipe Herrera's "Borderbus"—may be done primarily to give participants aesthetic and conceptual models for their work, but any discussion in this area can lead to pointed and heated discussions, which library professionals should feel reasonably well-prepared to manage before introducing material on such a fraught but urgent topic.[24]

One of the most influential books of the past several decades that has taken on the ways in which borders do not simply appear in landscapes but become a part of us on a cultural and psychic level is Gloria Anzaldúa's *Borderlands/La Frontera: The New Mestiza* (1987). Blurring the boundaries between autobiography and criticism, poetry and prose, Anzaldua's book offers ways to think how the conflicts of history have resulted in a tense, rich, polyglot present of indispensable hybridity:

> Cuando vives en la frontera
> people walk through you, the wind steals your voice,
> you're a burra, buey, scapegoat,
> forerunner of a new race,
> half and half—both woman and man, neither—
> a new gender;
>
> To live in the Borderlands means to
> put chile in the borscht,

eat whole wheat tortillas,
speak Tex Mex with a Brooklyn accent;
be stopped by la migra at the border checkpoints.[25]

Writing that sets itself the challenge of tracking how place is, as Doreen Massey earlier described it, "unfixed, contested, and multiple," are often looking for new forms, images, and frameworks to convey how things are mixed together and why this is necessary and exciting. Usually an exploration that moves along these lines is seeking to articulate hope about interdependence, unpredictability, and openness that can be elaborated and compounded as we research and write further into local and global spaces. We might offer the preceding passage from Anzaldúa alongside an excerpt from the concluding essay to *A TransPacific Poetics* (2017), an anthology that appeared thirty years later. The poet and editor Sawako Nakayasu proposes a way of thinking that echoes and extends the sentiment we find in Anzaldúa, while relocating us from figure to ground or, rather, to the ocean. Guided by a single conditional premise—"If water is the new bridge"—Nakayasu envisions a momentum for future writing in which "the new imperative is no longer just to traverse some definable locale, but to live, swim, dive, puncture, excavate, recuperate, rearticulate some new, fluid passionate flight over and beyond the old boundaries, to carry forward past and ongoing histories of place, space, adamantly local geology and ecology, sometimes it is wet, no longer is it linear, singular or limited to a single geography, identity, notion of centrality."[26]

A description that feels enticing, in part because it is a little dizzying, can be useful to spur on the sort of writing a reader wants to see in the world, which is what writers should feel empowered to pursue. You should encourage participants to take Anzaldúa and Nakayasu as broadly as they want. If they are unsure whether or not any particular place is speaking to them on this level, perhaps there is another part of an existing or unwritten project that can be thought of more usefully as a topography than as a stubborn object. A line of poetry or dialogue, like a character's motivations, might be things we try to imagine rotating, folding, contorting, or stretching into different shapes. Thinking about space more critically, as an active element on the page and in the world, will, with any luck, assist in this.

Notes

1. Yi-Fu Tuan, *Space and Place: The Perspective of Experience* (University of Minnesota Press, 1977), 4.

2. Doreen Massey, *Space, Place and Gender* (Polity, 1994), 5.

3. Rebecca Solnit, *Encyclopedia of Trouble and Spaciousness* (Trinity University Press, 2014), 1.

4. Moshim Hamid, *Exit West* (Riverhead Books 2017), 72.

5. See S. I. Hayakawa, *Language in Thought and Action* (Paw Prints, 2008), 84.

6. Virginia Woolf, *Selected Essays* (Oxford University Press, 2009), 178.

7. Stacy Szymaszek, *Journal of Ugly Sites and Other Journals* (Fence Books, 2016), 80.

8. 92nd Street Y, "Nathaniel Mackey and Cathy Park Hong with New York High-School Students" (July 14, 2016), https://www.youtube.com/watch?v=4uUUAWV1ENE.

9. Hannah Arendt, *The Human Condition* (Doubleday Anchor Books, 1959), 227–28.

10. Rachel Carson, *The Sea Around Us* (Oxford University Press, 1951), 75.

11. Larry Levis, *The Selected Levis* (University of Pittsburgh Press, 2003), 135.

12. Alice Munro, *Selected Stories* (Vintage, 1997), 40.

13. Christine Schutt, *A Day, A Night, Another Day, Summer* (Harcourt, 2005), 137.

14. Neal Ascherson, "The Borderlands," *Granta* (February 2, 1990), https://granta.com/the-borderlands/.

15. Eavan Boland, *In a Time of Violence* (W.W. Norton, 1995), 7.

16. Christine Smallwood, "Back Talk: Toni Morrison," *The Nation* (November 19, 2008), https://www.thenation.com/article/back-talk-toni-morrison/.

17. William Cronon, *Changes in the Land: Indians, Colonists, and the Ecology of New England* (Hill and Wang, 2003), 19.

18. Toni Morrison, *A Mercy* (Knopf, 2008), 9.

19. Jeffrey Brown, "'Writing Out of a Loneliness,' Novelists Explore the Range of Native Experiences," *PBS Newshour* (July 26, 2018), https://www.pbs.org/newshour/show/writing-out-of-a-loneliness-novelist-explores-the-range-of-native-experiences.

20. Sinclair Lewis, *It Can't Happen Here* (Penguin, 2014), 22–23.

21. Marilynne Robinson, *Housekeeping* (Farrar, Straus and Giroux, 2004), 90–92.

22. Claire-Louise Bennett, *Pond* (Riverhead, 2017), 24–26.

23. Lynda Barry, *Cruddy* (Simon & Schuster, 1999), 3.

24. Juan Felipe Herrera, "Borderbus," The Poetry Foundation, https://www .poetryfoundation.org/poems/91751/borderbus; Seamus Heaney, *The Haw Lantern* (Farrar, Straus and Giroux, 2014), 6.

25. Gloria Anzaldúa, *Borderlands/La Frontera: The New Mestiza* (Aunt Lute Books, 2007), 216.

26. Lisa Samuels and Sawako Nakayasu, eds., *A TransPacific Poetics* (Litmus, 2017), 186.

8

Poetry and Verse

Early in the summer of 2017, poetry was in the news. Specifically, the findings of a National Endowment for the Arts (NEA) survey had just elaborated a simple, affirming fact: more adults were reading poetry. Almost twice as many were reading poems as surveys had recorded in 2012, with rates increasing most sharply for young adults (ages 18–24) and nonwhite populations.[1] Some national news outlets had started to openly acknowledge their struggles to find more hopeful material during the previous months. A story about poetry drawing more readers certainly felt optimistic, or at least different from the day's other stories, sketching details of Reality Winner's arrest, the resignation of the U.S. ambassador to China, and the revised number of fatalities from the previous week's bombing in Kabul, the deadliest since 2001.

While commentators might speculate as to why and how this change had taken place (Do tumultuous times naturally draw people to poetry? Is the triviality of social media having the same effect?), as librarians, we are in the more appealing position of deciding what to do with a gift. While we may or may not be surprised by these findings based on observations in our own library settings, we can do more than just hope that this enthusiasm will continue. Librarians should be considering how poetry provides a particular opportunity for both engaging existing patrons and bringing new faces into the mix. Of course, it is still worth remembering that while 43 percent of adults in a 2015 NEA study reported reading a work of literature during the previous year, the newly sky-high percentage of adults reading poetry in 2017 remained just under 12 percent. So while poetry readership has enjoyed substantial increases, that it remains marginalized is all the more reason to consider our own presumptions and attitudes about it as readers and library professionals more closely. The fact is that even many people who consider themselves to be lovers of books will openly admit to hating poetry. At the very least, many readers who devour large quantities of fiction or nonfiction have decided, at some point or another, that verse is simply not for them. To them, poetry is recondite, excessive, affected, or just bewildering.

That we, as readers and writers, have never known quite what to make of poetry is, of course, one of its chief virtues. It is slippery, like the human mind. We fall under its spell. Mina Loy describes poetry as "prose bewitched," whereas William Carlos Williams famously stated that "poetry is a machine made of words." There is no need to choose between these definitions. While it is possible to pursue writing prompts with a grounding in traditional poetic forms conditioned by rhyme and meter, it is also possible to start by encouraging patrons to explore the ways in which poetry can happen by chance, as an event rooted in exploratory play. The radical experiments of the Dadaists a little more than a century ago are now part of the canon of procedures for making a poem, and they are easily shared with writers with varying levels of experience.

 The Cut-Up Technique

Instead of throwing out old newspapers and periodicals from your library, you can collect them for the following poetry activities. Tristan Tzara gave very simple instructions, quoted here, for how to "make a Dadaist poem," which is to say, by chance:

- Take a newspaper.
- Take a pair of scissors.
- Choose an article as long as you are planning to make your poem.
- Cut out the article.
- Then cut out each of the words that make up this article and put them in a bag.
- Shake it gently.
- Then take out the scraps one after the other in the order in which they left the bag.
- Copy conscientiously.
- The poem will be like you.
- And here you are a writer, infinitely original and endowed with a sensibility that is charming, though beyond the understanding of the vulgar.[2]

If your participants would like to be more deliberate with their cut-up techniques, you may try modifying Tzara's method:

- Take a newspaper or periodical.
- Cut out each word or phrase that strikes you, being sure to include verbs as well as nouns.
- Arrange them intuitively/consciously, and then copy your poem.

You may even modify this more deliberate approach by assigning parameters to how the words and phrases are chosen and arranged:

- Cut out every word or phrase that might pertain to or describe animals.
- Arrange them using ten syllables per line, adding your own words where necessary.

One reason for working at such an explicitly physical level with language is to be as hands-on as possible about how poetic sense gets made. Writers can be invited to try out combinatory possibilities within an already existing set of words and phrases, rearranging them to create distinct strings of meaning (or gibberish). Pieces of language can be treated more like parts of a puzzle when they have not been generated by the writer's own hand. Since the resulting arrangements will feel more contingent or provisional (the writer just happened to pull them from a bag in that order, or to place one next to the other), they can also be reworked, remaining mobile and open to revision. "Sense" arises, but context also counts. Sense is never just one thing and it can always be deferred, thwarted, or suspended. Part of what defines poetry is its exaggerated capacity to make what Robert Frost calls "the sound of sense," or to proceed by linking and deflecting what Stephanie Burt calls "close calls with nonsense."

# Nonsense Verse

Nonsense verse has a long history, and its popular practitioners have included Edward Lear, Lewis Carroll, and Dr. Seuss, any one of whom could be used as a model for your participants to write their own nonsense verse. Here are some ideas for getting started, using Carroll's "Jabberwocky" and a nonsense vocabulary.

- Begin by reading Lewis Carroll's "Jabberwocky," which can be found online.
- Ask your participants what feelings and situations it evokes and how.
- Have your participants replace each of Carroll's nonsense words with a real word and share the results.
- Then have your participants brainstorm their own, original nonsense words and use at least ten of them to create a new poem.
- Finally, you can have your participants replace their own nonsense words with real words and see what happens.

Here is another exercise using "The Jumblies" and nonsense creatures:

- Begin by reading Edward Lear's "The Jumblies," which can be found online.
- Ask your participants to recount and share all the characteristics of the Jumblies.

▓ Have your participants name a creature or creatures of their own and brainstorm their attributes.

▓ Finally, have your participants write a new poem about their nonsense creature(s). ⬟⬟⬟

While writing that flirts with or fully embraces nonsense offers one way of thinking about and experiencing the musicality of language traditionally associated with poetry, sometimes it is difficult to identify a poem when you're looking right at one. In the first place, many of them look precisely like prose. Unlike the famous Supreme Court Justice Potter Stewart writing about identifying pornography, you will not necessarily "know it when [you] see it." Indeed, as Walt Whitman drafted the lines that would later constitute *Leaves of Grass,* he didn't, at first, feel that it was poetry he was creating. He thought he might be writing a new kind of oratory to try out on the lecture circuit, and when Whitman sent his first edition of *Leaves of Grass* to Ralph Waldo Emerson, Emerson referred to it not as poetry but as "wit and wisdom." This was a generic description that Whitman would feel the need to correct in his letter back to Emerson, in which he mentions "poems," "poets," or "poetry" thirty-three times, seven in the first paragraph alone.

A contemporary example of this kind of multiplicity can be seen in the work of Claudia Rankine who, after publishing three previous collections of poetry, added a subtitle to her book *Don't Let Me Be Lonely: An American Lyric* (2004). Continuing her work at the intersection of poetry and essay, she retained the designation of "lyric" for her much-lauded *Citizen: An American Lyric* (2014) about violence and microaggressions against African Americans in the United States. Though written without any verse lineation, this work was a National Book Critics Circle Award finalist for both poetry *and* criticism in 2014. (It won for poetry). While it is striking in some ways that a major literary award would so openly acknowledge the porous boundary between genres, writers have long been aware of how artificial such demarcations can be. Many prefer a both/and approach that institutions can be reluctant to recognize. We might be better off contenting ourselves with a durable definition of poetry as an event tied to reading. In an 1870 letter that Emily Dickinson wrote to Thomas Wentworth Higginson, she puts it as follows: "If I read a book and it makes my whole body so cold no fire can warm me I know that is poetry. If I feel physically as if the top of my head were taken off, I know that is poetry. These are the only ways I know it. Is there any other way?"

No doubt there are, but let's stick with this idea of poetry as an encounter with something startling, disconcerting, or transportive. Something that makes us slow down and attend to strangeness. We might imagine the writer's job as that of bringing material that activates this experience onto the page, but how does this happen? In the traditional picture a moment of deep inspiration occurs, one of inwardness, often guided by an animating muse. Part of what defined modernity, though, was the possibility of seeing the poetic process at work in the street, where the noise, spectacle, and physical detritus of the world were just as likely to be transformed in the poetic process. Poets, whether in the streets or the library stacks, were increasingly aware that they were pursuing something that depended on reception and framing. For many, poetic creation depended on an ability to recognize what was standing in front of them, and then having some strategies for how to set it apart from the cacophony of the world just enough for it to sing.

The Made And Re-Made

The wider traditions associated with found poetry offer one view of how the interactions between libraries, research, and poetic composition have been explored in the past and up to the present. Another way of putting these ideas into practice which can work at the time scale of a single afternoon is the scavenger hunt, which can serve as a tangible way to both stimulate creativity and begin or extend the process of familiarizing patrons with your library's resources and collections:

- Introduce your participants to examples of found poetry, like an excerpt from Kenneth Goldsmith's *Day*, a transcription of the September 11, 2001 edition of the *New York Times*.[3]

- Discuss what a found poem can do. What new meaning is added when Goldsmith repurposes the *Times* as poetry?
- Send your participants on a timed scavenger hunt through your library for found poetry. Share the results.

The Remix

- Have your participants remix or rearrange the language in their found poems, either consciously or by chance.

The Mash-Up

- Have your participants combine and remix two found poems. They can do this individually or in pairs.

The Erasure

- Have your participants make a new poem by erasing words in their found text. You may need black markers or white-out, or participants can just erase words by scratching them out with a pen.

In addition to these sorts of workshop-oriented activities, library staff may also want to consider a wider set of ideas for programming centered on the generation and performance of poetry that doesn't require a Ph.D. in literature to create. One of the challenges for both programming and collecting within libraries is to consider how the widespread popularity of an Internet poet like Rupi Kaur is coinciding with well-established contemporary poets of the print persuasion like Mary Oliver or Eileen Myles. The reading public that exists for poetry is lively, in part, because of the sharply diverging aesthetics that make programming for this group an interesting challenge. The robustness of poetry's reading audience is often matched by its writing community. While many of its readers and writers likely already enjoy your library's resources, without too much effort you can grow your user base by more explicitly catering to the secret or not-so-secret poets in all of us.

COLLECTING FOR POETS

Poetry tends to be among the more neglected areas of collection development in public libraries. Too often, library branches may have a smattering of canonical poets like Robert Frost and Maya Angelou, or those whose volumes also sit on the shelves at Target, almost hidden in their stacks. Poetry tends to circulate well, though, during National Poetry Month in April, when librarians call attention to it through special displays and exhibitions. A few ways to enhance and highlight poetry collections follow.

We should try to include the voices of the many living poets who are continuing to innovate the practice and captivate audiences. Libraries might start by making sure they have works by the present U.S. poet laureate and advertise these by putting them on display. Important poetry presses to collect include the likes of Farrar Straus and Giroux, Norton, Ecco, and Knopf, but

PRESSES WHOSE POETRY TO COLLECT

- BOA Editions
- Carcanet Press
- City Lights Publisher
- Cleveland State University Poetry Center
- Cleveland State University Press
- Coffee House Press
- Copper Canyon Press
- Ecco Press
- Faber & Faber (British)
- Farrar, Straus and Giroux
- Fence Books
- Four Way Books
- Graywolf Press
- Houghton Mifflin
- Kelsey Street Press
- Knopf Doubleday
- Letter Machine Editions
- Milkweed Editions
- New Directions Books
- Nightboat Books
- Penguin Random House
- Sarabande Books
- Soft Skull Press
- The Song Cave
- Tarpaulin Sky Press
- Ugly Duckling Presse
- University of Iowa Press
- W.W. Norton
- Wave Books
- Wesleyan University Press
- Yale University Press

NOTE: Some of the presses cited above are most readily obtained through the University Press of New England, Consortium Book Sales and Distribution, and Small Press Distribution, three larger organizations which are particularly strong resources for poetry.[4]

also smaller, independent presses such as Copper Canyon Press, Wave Books, Graywolf Press, and Sarabande Books. Monitoring Small Press Distribution's monthly poetry bestseller list could provide an easy guide for the collector who wants to expand her purview.[5] University presses such as Wesleyan University Press, Princeton University Press, and the University of Iowa Press also have important poetry lines.

Moreover, there are major competition winners that will enrich readers' ideas about poetry in the here and now. The Academy of American Poets awards several important prizes in the field, including the prestigious Wallace Stevens Award, the Lenore Marshall Poetry Prize, the James Laughlin Award, and the Walt Whitman Award. The Yale Series of Younger Poets is still depended on to identify new talent in the field. One may want to start with the larger prizes that garner more press coverage, though. Libraries may, for instance, create special displays for past Pulitzer Prize winners in poetry, and for Nobel Prize or MacArthur "Genius Grant" winners who are poets when those prizes are annually awarded and publicized in the popular press. Other awards to look for include the National Book Critics Circle Awards, the National Book Awards, and our own American Library Association/Reference & User Services Association's (ALA/RUSA) annual Notable Books List.

POETRY COMPETITION WINNERS TO COLLECT

- Griffin Poetry Prize
- Iowa Poetry Prize
- James Laughlin Award
- Lenore Marshall Poetry Prize
- National Book Award in Poetry
- National Book Critics Circle Award in Poetry
- National Poetry Series
- Pulitzer Prize in Poetry
- Wallace Stevens Award
- Walt Whitman Award
- Whiting Award in Poetry
- Yale Series of Younger Poets

These suggestions are by no means exhaustive, and to find influential poets in the United States, librarians should branch out from presses and prizes to more popular spaces like Twitter, Instagram, and Beyoncé albums to find the poets with perhaps the largest followings, such as Patricia Lockwood, Warsan Shire, and Morgan Parker. Regardless, the first and best place to begin serving poets is by amping up your library's poetry collection and promoting it.

POETRY ANTHOLOGIES TO COLLECT

- *The Ecco Anthology of International Poetry*
- *Technicians of the Sacred*
- *The BreakBeat Poets* (vols. 1–2)
- *Legitimate Dangers: American Poets of the New Century*
- *Poems for the Millennium* (vols. 1–4)
- *The Making of a Poem: A Norton Anthology of Poetic Forms*
- *American Poets in the 21st Century: The New Poetics*
- *American Women Poets in the 21st Century*
- *Troubling the Line: Trans and Genderqueer Poetry and Poetics*
- *The New Census: An Anthology of Contemporary American Poetry*
- *A TransPacific Poetics*
- *Another Republic*
- *The Norton Anthology of Poetry*
- *The Vintage Book of American Poetry*
- *A Book of Luminous Things: An International Anthology of Poetry*
- *The Penguin Anthology of Twentieth-Century American Poetry*

PROGRAMMING FOR POETS

Reading Series/Open Mic Night

There are probably more practicing poets in your service area than you realize, and a reading series or open mic night is one way to bring them out of hiding. The difference between a reading series and an open mic night is that the lineup for a reading series is set in advance, whereas open mic nights welcome any participants who would like to perform during or on the night of the actual event. Reading series might be better for library branches in or near larger cities that have more readers to draw from. Examples of successful reading series put on by public libraries include the BONK! Performance Series at the Racine Public Library, the Aural Literature Series at the Austin Public Library, and the Public Library of Cincinnati and Hamilton County's Poetry in the Garden series. An open mic night, however, can give librarians more of a sense of the scope of practicing poets who live in their service area.

Hosting either an open mic night or a reading series requires an accommodating event space (with a microphone setup and seating) and a little bit of planning and marketing. Unless your reading series features well-known or famous poets, attendance at open mic events will probably be greater. A reading series, however, allows you to plan ahead and keep greater control over the event. You may, of course, program both; you can begin with a series of open mic events as a way to survey the user base of practicing poets in your service area, then invite those participants back to perform as part of a more structured reading series.

Do poets actually enjoy reading their poetry aloud? In the first place, what you'll likely find is that many of your readers will not merely be poets who read their written work to an audience, but poets whose work *requires* an audience. In slam poetry and spoken word performance, the utterance of the poetry is part of the piece, and regional and national slam championships frequently garner large, participatory audiences. Without being overly prescriptive about audience participation, it makes sense to set out some guidelines in advance, such as politely finger-snapping at good lines rather than applauding or whooping. Slam, spoken word, and other performance-based poetries, including American Sign Language poetry, all have long and rich histories and should be encouraged in your series.

AMERICAN SIGN LANGUAGE LITERATURE

American Sign Language (ASL) is widely used in the United States. According to the Gallaudet Research Institute, anywhere from 9 to 22 persons out of 1,000 in the United States have a severe hearing impairment or are deaf. Depending on the circumstances of their impairment, such patrons may primarily comunicate through ASL, which is a visual language that relies primarily on the shape, movement, and placing of the hands ("signing"). Thus, most ASL signers learn to read written English but may consider it a second language. Deafness is a cultural identity, and ASL has its own rich history of recorded, performed, oral literature.

Gallaudet University Libraries provides a handy LibGuide for ASL literature.[6] Its "Selected Bibliography" suggests a number of foundational texts in Deaf storytelling and poetry.

Major Works of ASL Poetry

- Clayton Valli, *ASL Poetry: Selected Works of Clayton Valli* (San Diego, CA: Dawn Pictures, 1995). Clayton Valli is a linguist and foundational ASL poet whose work has helped legitimize ASL poetry as a valid and recognized form of artistic expression.

- Ben Bahan and Sam Supalla, *Bird of a Different Feather and for a Decent Living* (1994). Ben Bahan is a professor of ASL and Deaf studies at Gallaudet University. He is a foundational figure in ASL storytelling, as is his colleague, the linguist Sam Supalla. From the publisher's description: "This book is a metaphor for how the Deaf have been treated throughout history, and the empowerment they find amongst their own. Told through the eyes of a little eaglet born with a straight beak instead of curved, Bahan draws a clear parallel between the mistreatment of Deaf people and child abuse."

- Dorothy Miles, *Gestures A: Poetry by Dorothy Miles* (Acton, CA: Joyce Media, 1976). Dorothy Miles is an important ASL poet and activist, both in the United States and the United Kingdom. Her poetry in ASL is among the most widely imitated.

- *Heart of the Hydrogen Jukebox* (Rochester, NY: Rochester Institute of Technology, 2008). This anthology is an important, wide-ranging review of ASL literature. From the publisher's description: "This celebration of American Sign Language poetry traces its development and includes interviews with poets and clips of historic poetry performances. Poets include: Robert Panara, Bernard Bragg,

Dorothy Miles, Patrick Graybill, Ella Mae Lentz, Clayton Valli, Peter Cook, Jim Cohn, Allen Ginsberg, and Debbie Rennie. Performances include: 1st National ASL Poetry Conference; Bridge of . . . ; Flying Words Project; and Rookie Night."

■ Ella Mae Lentz, *The Treasure: Poems by Ella Mae Lentz* (San Diego, CA: In Motion, 1996). Ella Mae Lentz is an important Deaf American poet and activist. Like Dorothy Miles, she is a key figure in ASL literature. Like much ASL literature, this collection provides commentary on what it means to be Deaf and the importance of ASL as a means of communication and identity.

The difficulty with organizing an open mic event is that you never know what you're going to get. You might have low attendance, or you might have too many performers for an hour-long event. You also don't know whether your performers' pieces will contain triggering, offensive, or culturally insensitive material (you'd be surprised how often this is the case). Thus, you may want to set ground rules ahead of time and clearly advertise them before the start of the event. For an hour-long event, rules might include the following: the event will be capped at the first ten performers who sign up, and they will perform for no longer than five minutes apiece; the library will not tolerate language that threatens or discriminates against anyone based on social categories such as race/ethnicity, country of origin, gender, sexual orientation, age, or abilities; and audience members should finger-snap quietly for encouragement during the performance, but hold their applause until after the end of each performance. You can find many open mic rules online, but you should adapt them to your own purposes and align them with your library's other standards and practices, including whether performers will be allowed to mention triggering events such as sexual assaults, eating disorders, or violent situations.

A reading series differs from an open mic event insofar as generally there are fewer readers reading for longer stretches of time, and they're readers whom presumably you've vetted and invited to read. Thirty to forty-five minutes of reading time is standard, divided among one to four readers, and fifteen minutes can be left for questions from the audience or book signings. Again, these events tend to draw smaller crowds than open mics, but have fewer variables. Open mics also tend to draw a younger crowd, and in particular, your young-adult user base might come out in fuller force than for a reading series.

Massive Open Online Courses

Massive open online courses (MOOCs) are relatively new phenomena. MOOCs are free, online courses designed for international audiences of lifelong learners and are generally delivered out of American universities. They're also perfect for libraries! And they're great as well to use for organizing poetry-writing groups. MOOCs such as Al Filreis's "Modern and Contemporary American Poetry" (or "ModPo"), Elisa New's "Poetry in America," Robert Pinsky's "The Art of Poetry," or the MOOC poetry-writing series out of the University of Iowa's International Writing Program are, for the most part, half-term (six to eight-week) courses aimed at general audiences that explore the history of the practice of poetry in America and beyond. How might they work for organizing a writing group? Most of the MOOCs are organized by week or module, and often release their content weekly or biweekly, and that's if you're taking the course in real time as it happens, rather than working from a course that has already passed but has been archived by the respective platform (Coursera, EdX, HarvardX, etc.).

Librarians could go a couple of routes with using MOOCs for writing groups: (1) using writing group meeting times to view and read the course content as a group; or (2) assigning the course content as "homework" and meeting as a group to discuss and supplement it. In general, the course content for each week or module is manageable and designed to take no more than two or three hours per week of the users' time. Most weeks and modules contain no more than a half-hour of video content on a handful of poems that are available online. If you choose to watch the video content as a group, you will obviously need a meeting space with a projector hooked up to an online computer. Likewise, if you choose to read the poems as a group, you will need to print them out for your participants. Some poetry MOOCs like the University of Iowa's "How Writers Write Poetry" or Pinsky's "The Art of Poetry" are more geared to discussions of craft and the generation of new work than other MOOCs, like Filreis's or New's, which are more historically and conceptually focused. Thus, Iowa's MOOCs come with their own poetry prompts for users, and librarians could use their group meeting times as studio hours for participants to explore the prompts and share their results. Discussions in MOOCs (such as those of Filreis and New) can also be easily adapted into poetry prompts for emerging writers. If "ModPo" is discussing appropriated (found) poetry one week, you can use the prompts for found poetry discussed earlier in this chapter, or you can make your own. If "Poetry in America" is discussing how Emily Dickinson engaged with the politics of her time, your prompt for your participants could be to write a poem that engages with contemporary politics (perhaps obliquely through descriptions of parlor objects).

It's exciting to organize a writing group around the MOOCs as they happen, because many of them have their own discussion

POETRY MOOCS

- "The Art of Poetry" (Boston University via EdX)
- "How to Make a Poem" (Manchester Metropolitan University via FutureLearn)
- "How Writers Write Poetry," "Power of the Pen: Identities and Social Issues in Poetry and Plays," "#Flashwrite Teen Poetry MOOC," and other University of Iowa MOOCs (University of Iowa via NovoEd)
- "Modern American Poetry" (University of Illinois–Urbana/Champaign via Coursera)
- "Modern and Contemporary American Poetry" (University of Pennsylvania via Coursera, typically runs annually from early September to late November)
- "Poetry in America" (Harvard University via HarvardX)
- "Sharpened Visions: A Poetry Workshop" (California Institute of the Arts via Coursera)

boards full of illuminating insights that make users feel part of a broader community. Moreover, there are often course hashtags that allow users to connect with each other over social media. The courses are also archived after they've been delivered, which gives you, the librarian, the opportunity to curate the MOOC content to fit the purposes of your writing group.

GENERATING POEMS

Generative Reading Workshop

One way to bring new poems into the library is to start a generative reading workshop. In this format, you meet as a group to read a poem or a short, curated collection of poems by a particular writer with an eye to what that writer pays attention to and how he or she might have generated the poem(s) that are being discussed. Have your reading group brainstorm things they noticed about the poem(s):

- Is there a particular mood or tone?
- Are there recurring themes?
- Are there recurring images?
- What's happening with the sound-play: rhyme, rhythm, alliteration, assonance, consonance, and so on?

Once your group has read the poem(s) and is done brainstorming, give them fifteen to thirty minutes, depending on your time constraints, to produce their own, original poems in the fashion of the poem(s) they've just read. Did the author use an ABAB rhyme scheme? Then perhaps your group will try out an ABAB rhyme scheme. Was the poetry somber? Have them write somber poems. Was the poetry largely about nature? Have them write somber nature poems using an ABAB rhyme scheme. Imitation, after all, is largely poets' first avenue to new work, and it's an excuse to read cool poems to boot!

If you're looking for a shortcut, the poet Kenneth Koch produced a book, *Rose, Where Did You Get That Red? Teaching Great*

Poetry to Children (1973), that enumerates prompts fashioned from reading "great poems" and imitating their most salient qualities. The title of the book comes from a child's poem imitating William Blake's "The Tyger" by asking questions of a rose. Blake's poem generates and proceeds by asking of "The Tyger" how it was made:

> Tyger Tyger, burning bright,
> In the forests of the night;
> What immortal hand or eye,
> Could frame thy fearful symmetry?

From such a procedure, one of Koch's school-aged students produced the following:

> Dog, where did you get that bark?
> Dragon, where do you get that flame?
> Kitten, where did you get that meow?
> Rose, where did you get that red?
> Bird, where did you get those wings?[7]

Koch published two subsequent books, *Sleeping on the Wing* (1981) and *Making Your Own Days* (1999), which may be equally useful to consult for poems and prompts for writers at any level.

Notebooking

Before Whitman began drafting what came to be *Leaves of Grass,* he notebooked. He carried his notebooks with him around New York City, composing lines that might or might not be included in his later, published work. One can even see the bumps in his handwriting from when he was notebooking in the omnibus and the vehicle would hit a stone or impediment. Notebooking takes the pressure off the poet to produce a poem in full when she sits down to write. By collecting words, phrases, lines, and images as they occur to the writer, or by having planned notebooking sessions, the poet is priming the pump for further acts of gathering, the composition of something from scratch, or the act of working through, rearranging, and adding to the bank of verbiage her notebook contains. Whitman isn't the only poet who notebooked. George Oppen's

Daybooks are often as compelling as his published poems. Stephen Kuusisto, Deborah Tall, and David Weiss have even compiled a compendium of excerpts from the notebooks of poets such as Rita Dove, Joy Harjo, James Merrill, and others in *The Poet's Notebook: Excerpts from the Notebooks of 26 American Poets* (1997). What if you haven't got a notebook? Happily, one doesn't need a notebook to notebook. The contemporary poet Lauren Haldeman, for instance, kept a list of poetic phrases that her toddler daughter said as she was learning to speak on a Twitter account. Then Haldeman used that list to produce a whole section of her second collection of poems, *Instead of Dying* (2017). This is one example of how the purposes of the poetic notebook overlap with some of those in life-writing.

You may begin your writing group by having your participants free-write or notebook for a timed five minutes. The idea is not to be self-conscious about what is being written but to let one's writerly mind and attentions wander freely. It helps to launch your group's free-writing session with a simple prompt, which may be just a list of words: tanager, infant, indigo, friendly fire, levitate; or it may be a question: *What would the walls of your childhood bedroom say?* or, *List every red thing you saw today.*

Listing

That last prompt might produce a whole poem. The list or catalog poem has its own long tradition. As mentioned previously, an epic poem like Homer's *Iliad* contains a Catalogue of Ships that identifies the various contingents of the Greek army that sailed to Troy. In Whitman's epic poem "Song of Myself," the occupations of individuals are of interest:

> The pure contralto sings in the organ loft,
> The carpenter dresses his plank, the tongue of his foreplane whistles its wild ascending lisp,
> The married and unmarried children ride home to their Thanksgiving dinner,
> The pilot seizes the king-pin, he heaves down with a strong arm,
> The mate stands braced in the whale-boat, lance and harpoon are ready,

> The duck-shooter walks by silent and cautious stretches,
> The deacons are ordain'd with cross'd hands at the altar,
> The spinning-girl retreats and advances to the hum of the big wheel,
> The farmer stops by the bars as he walks on a First-day loafe and looks at the oats and rye

For Whitman, America's "Catalogue of Ships" is its lay citizenry employed in their daily activities, but elsewhere he tweaks the conceit of the catalog by merely listing sounds.[8] The tradition of the catalog or list extends into contemporary practice as well. Inger Christensen's *Alphabet* proceeds by naming objects in sections corresponding to respective letters of the alphabet (1 = A, 2 = B, etc.) followed, intermittently, by the verb *exist(s)*:

> 3
>
> cicadas exist; chicory, chromium
> citrus trees; cicadas exist;
> cicadas, cedars, cypresses, the cere-
> bellum[9]

List or catalog poems are relatively easy to make using simple prompts or parameters. You can have your participants make poems by listing things that are a particular color. Other possible prompts or constraints include the following:

- List things a bird might think.
- List things that are fluid, liquid, or colloidal.
- List things that make you think of a particular person.
- List made-up names of dog breeds.
- List all the things you see on your way to work or school.

Exquisite Corpse

Exquisite Corpse began as a popular game among French surrealist that was aimed at getting the creative juices flowing by thwarting intentionality. In the more common American variant, the participants each begin with a piece of paper on which they write a line of poetry. Then the papers are passed clockwise or counterclockwise, and the next participant reads the previous line, folds it over so that it will no longer be visible, and adds a line of his or her own. That way, for each pass, only the preceding line is visible to the new author. Once the poems have made it all the way around the table or parlor, the paper is unfolded and the poem is read in full.

Constraints

In 1969, Georges Perec wrote a 300-page novel without using the letter *e*. His novel, translated into English as *A Void* (2012) remains one of the landmark works from a group of French writers and mathematicians who produced experimental literature using hyper-specific and often outlandish strictures. Their group was called Oulipo, and they used constraints to liberate their imaginations from the traps of intentionality in order to inspire new and fresh work. The Oulipean tradition continues today with poets like Christian Bök, whose book *Eunoia* (2001) comprises five chapters, each of which is written using only a single vowel. Here's an excerpt from Chapter A:

> A pagan skald chants a dark saga (a Mahabharata), as a papal
>   cabal blackballs all
> annals and tracts, all dramas and psalms: Kant and Kafka,
>   Marx and Marat. A law as harsh as a fatwa bans all
>   paragraphs that lack an A as a standard hallmark.[10]

Omitting certain letters from use in a text makes it a "lipogram." Another example of a lipogram using only the letter *a* (thus omitting *e, i, o, u*) is Cathy Park Hong's "Ballad in A," which begins: "A Kansan plays cards, calls Marshall / a crawdad, that barb lands that rascal a slap; / that Kansan jackass scats, / camps back at caballada ranch."[11] Of course, working with rhyme, meter, and other traditional elements provides its own constraints. If those aren't your group's cups of tea, you can make up your own constraints in the tradition of Oulipo:

- Make a poem shaped like a DNA molecule, in which the beginning and ending letters of each line are A-T or C-G pairs.

- Write a poem in which every noun begins with an *x*. (You might begin by brainstorming nouns that begin with *x*, or by making dictionaries available.)
- Write a five-to-ten-word poem in which each word contains one more letter than the previous one.
- Write a ten-line poem using your phone number to determine the number of syllables per line.

ELECTIVE AFFINITIES

There are many other examples of library programming for poets, from special displays to Twitter hashtags for National Poetry Month (April). The Shaler North Hills Library in Pennsylvania, among others, prints poems for patrons and puts them on display for takeaway during National Poem in Your Pocket Day, for which occasion the Academy of American Poets publishes an easily downloadable packet of poems.[12] For Valentine's Day, valentines can be made of poems, canonical or original, or you can send your patrons on a "blind date" with poetry by wrapping a book of poems, concealing its title and author, and identifying it only with a card using language in the style of a personals ad. Such programming encourages reading or sharing already written poetry. For poetry production itself, the above suggestions are only the tip of the iceberg. Graywolf Press's *The Art of* _____ series, including *The Art of the Poetic Line* by James Longenbach and *The Art of Recklessness* by Dean Young, as well as *The Triggering Town: Lectures and Essays on Poetry and Writing* by Richard Hugo, are also robust resources.

Librarians and poets have long shared affinities, which may be why so many poets have become librarians, including Philip Larkin and the former librarian of Congress, Archibald MacLeish. As stewards of the practice, librarians should remember MacLeish's words about libraries, for they pertain equally to poems: "What is more important in a library than anything else—than everything else—is the fact that it exists." Ditto poems.

Notes

1. Sunil Iyengar, "Taking Note: Poetry Reading Is Up—Federal Survey Results," National Endowment for the Arts (June 7, 2018), https://www.arts .gov/art-works/2018/taking-note-poetry-reading-%E2%80%94federal-survey -results.

2. Tristan Tzara, "How to Make a Dadaist Poem," University of Pennsylvania, https://www.writing.upenn.edu/~afilreis/88v/tzara.html.

3. Kenneth Goldsmith, "Day," poets.org, Academy of American Poets, https:// www.poets.org/poetsorg/poem/day-excerpt.

4. See UPNE Book Partners, https://www.upne.com/dist_services.html; Consortium Book Sales & Distribution, https://www.cbsd.com; and Small Press Distribution, https://www.spdbooks.org.

5. See "Poetry Bestsellers Archive," Small Press Distribution, https://www .spdbooks.org/pages/bestsellers/poetry/Poetry-Bestsellers-Archive.aspx.

6. "ASL Literature," Gallaudet University Library, http://libguides.gallaudet .edu/content.php?pid=225639.

7. Kenneth Koch, *Rose, Where Did You Get That Red? Teaching Great Poetry to Children* (New York, 1973).

8. Walt Whitman, *Song of Myself and Other Poems,* ed. Robert Hass (Berkeley, CA: Counterpoint, 2010), 83–84, 98.

9. Inger Christensen, *Alphabet* [excerpt], poets.org, Academy of American Poets, https://www.poets.org/poetsorg/poem/alphabet-excerpt.

10. Christian Bök, *Eunoia: The Upgraded Edition* (Coach House Books, 2005).

11. Cathy Park Hong, "Ballad in A," *Poetry Magazine* (April 2010), https://www .poetryfoundation.org/poetrymagazine/poems/53500/ballad-in-a.

12. "Poem in Your Pocket Day," Academy of American Poets, https://www .poets.org/sites/default/files/poempocketday_april_26_2018_f.pdf.

CONCLUSION

A founding premise of this book is that library users should be understood as writers and makers, that being a world citizen means having the right and the responsibility to express oneself, and that explorations of voice and perspective are part of this effort. This book frames libraries as places where skills and curiosities are shared and robustly supported. Creative writing provides a particular challenge, given that library resources can be used with an eye toward developing literary work in a range of genres. Using the library as a generative tool is a distinctive practice, and to support it, we close this book with guidance and commentary on pragmatic skills and concepts like information-seeking through interviewing and online searching, and copyright, that inevitably concern makers.

We give attention here to other aspects of hosting working writers in the library, too. For however much that writing depends on a willingness and an ability to sit down with a pen or at the keyboard, as a solitary individual committing thoughts to the page, there are important times when writing calls for interaction and exchange. Sometimes writers enjoy breaking free from their solitary work, and some rely on groups to provide feedback on their work in progress. While many aspects of writing practice are individual choices—morning or evening, pen and paper versus the computer keyboard, amid the society of a coffee shop or in the silence of one's study—the matters discussed here are ones which have established best practices.

One of these best practices is the process of seeking information to support one's writing. When people want to write, looking for facts to clarify a concept or details to enliven some aspect of a story can seem like a distraction. Yet writers need facts, as so many interviews with professional writers attest, and for every writer who feels stymied by research, there is one who is enthralled by it. For her historical novel *Manhattan Beach* (2017), Jennifer Egan drew on materials ranging from "Navy deep sea diving manuals from the 1940s . . . to literary classics" as part of her writing process.[1] The Pulitzer Prize-winner Anthony Doerr has recounted the halting, initial steps toward his novel *All the Light We Cannot See* (2014). During a fellowship to support his work on that novel, Doerr found himself pondering the distance between his ideas for a novel "about the French radio resistance" and the fact that he couldn't "speak French, [had] never operated an old radio, and [couldn't] imagine how a Frenchman might talk in 1940, or even what he might carry in his pockets." His memoir of that time recounts his disbelief that he, a new father, exhausted by young twins, could convert his collection of "grainy photos of bombed out cities" and everything he had read "about the Allied assault on Germany" into another novel.[2]

Guidance on how and where to search can make the information-seeking that is integral to writing more seamless with the work a writer wants to do. The advent of Google has made acquiring information seem easy: type a few words into the now iconic search box, and almost instantaneously thousands, if not millions, of results are produced. If a writer is lucky, the background she wants to refamiliarize herself with might appear, from an accurate and reputable source, in the first several search results. More often, it can take a fair amount of time to see if these results hold the desired information, and it might not be there at all. Knowing that the library's catalog can turn up *The Writer's Guide to Everyday Life in Regency and Victorian England* (1998), or that there are databases that allow a writer to see what it would cost to buy a loaf of bread in an earlier era, enables us to thread the needle.

We can enrich searchers' ideas about how to look for answers to the questions that emerge in the course of their writing projects through attention to both process and sources. Several concepts inform the way we can encourage writers to think about meeting their information needs:

> ***Search at small rather than at large:*** The language for this premise comes from Anne Fadiman's book *At Large and At Small: Familiar Essays* (2007). The simplest thing to do, when searching, is to search at large by turning to the massive information universe represented by Google or a "smart search" via a library's website. For many queries, though, we're better off searching "at small," or within a specialized website or a particular database. The latter option usually provides more relevant and more authoritative results, and we spend less time wading through irrelevant materials. Even when using Google, we can search a specific domain, for results in a particular language, and so on. All of these strategies help move us from the too-large world of the Internet's myriad sites to the experts and communities we are most interested in learning from.

> ***Search within specific fields:*** Think of the ways a single word can have different meanings. *Fielding* names both an eighteenth-century English novelist and a baseball skill. *Plants* can refer to organic life forms or to industrial facilities. *Green* is both a color and a relatively recent term to describe environmentally sound practices of living and working. *Apple* is simultaneously a fruit and a company name. Two well-known companies, actually, have used this name: the contemporary technology developer, and the record label that the Beatles founded in the late 1960s. If we search within a field—author name, corporate entity, and so on—we can increase the likelihood that our search results focus on the subject of interest to us, rather than the other ways the term might manifest. This search practice is one way of cutting down on the clutter of meaningless results, though admittedly, it's often not until you've run a search that you realize this problem.

Use Boolean logic: Google and many other search interfaces automatically and silently use what is technically known as Boolean logic. Most fundamentally, *Boolean logic* refers to the terms, essential in older, command-line searching, that allow searchers to combine or eliminate terms to formulate a search. These terms still structure our searches, and unless we opt for advanced search modes, Boolean logic sometimes can happen without our knowledge or control. The basic Boolean terms are AND, OR, and NOT. Aside from NOT, it's sometimes simplest to think about the terms' function as the opposite of the way they work in real life: AND creates more conditions for results, thereby limiting the number of items a researcher should evaluate, and OR loosens the restrictions on the search, creates options, and thus returns more results than a differently configured search would.

Understand literary warrant: Fans of *Downton Abbey* and other period dramas know that there's much scrutiny of characters' language: would someone have used that expression, or is it a later development? Is there a name for that distinctive style of dress? How did people talk about new inventions, whether the arrival of the telephone or the car? Another common example emerges when helping someone who is seeking more details about World War I from a contemporary perspective. In this search, you have to look for records of the Great War, because our term for that global conflict, World War I, depends on a second, then unknown conflict (World War II). These realities affect writers' information needs. As a researcher, you have two initial options in these cases. Looking at encyclopedia entries and related sources that offer overviews, along with suggested resources, is a good starting point. Another possibility would be to turn directly to a reputable primary source, like the *New York Times*, with its status as the newspaper of record, and browse within a date range to become familiar with the issues and vocabulary of the period.

Use finding aids: Accessing the materials in archives means using finding aids rather than a conventional library catalog. Most finding aids provide a brief overview of the subject's life and significance, as well as indicating how much material is available, but they typically do not offer an item-by-item inventory. This is particularly true of tools created in the era of the "more product, less process" philosophy to reduce archival backlogs and make material available to users.

LIBRARIES AND REMIX CULTURE: Some Programming Options

The concept of "remix culture," or using art or literature to create another medium or narrative, offers librarians another perspective on both intellectual property and the items in their collections. While we are expected to know copyright and to offer that expertise to less informed colleagues and patrons alike, the concept of the remix affords a more playful, less authoritarian take on the use of extant works. Writers for *Buzzfeed* took note of a November 2010 article in the *New York Times* that calls words "endlessly recyclable," a feature ensuring that "no harm can come from amateur writers trying their hand at using them."[3] How the library works as a generative tool in the era of remix culture will vary with literary form and technique. If you want to call library users' attention to the ways that work created by others can play a part in their own work, here are three illustrative pairs of program prompts.

1. *Nonfiction:* While the written accumulation of aphorisms and proverbs goes back much further, the keeping of commonplace books came to be recognized as a distinct and capacious practice during the fifteenth century. A commonplace book served as a place to recopy quotations, definitions, pieces of argument, poems, sermons, recipes, and tables of measurement, alongside a writer's own observations. While they functioned essentially as a hodgepodge, pragmatic way to contain information, they also played a crucial role in the work of many scientists and intellectuals, and in exceptional cases, such as Robert Burton's *Anatomy of Melancholy* (1621), they became enormous acts of

literature. Since modernism and its aftermath are held together by an interest in fragmentation, it is not difficult to find work that feels as though it updates the form of the commonplace book, sometimes perversely. You can share David Shields's "Life Story" (a first-person essay composed entirely from bumper-sticker slogans) as a way to discuss the difference between originality of language and originality of concept.[4]

2. *Fiction:* Libraries can and should provide spaces in which practitioners of fan fiction can congregate and share their work. Related programming might involve drawing on that community for a book club exploring other concepts of adaptation and parallel retellings in contemporary fiction. While the pair of novels chosen could vary widely depending on the interest of the group (*Bridget Jones' Diary* with *Pride and Prejudice* would be very different from *Wide Sargasso Sea* with *Jane Eyre*), the goal would be to consider other approaches for building fictional worlds that are in a dialogue with already existing narratives.

3. *Poetry:* While elements of collage are more widespread in contemporary poetry than traditional rhyme schemes, the cento has the virtue of being both literally ancient and strictly defined. Centos are composed exclusively from lines written by others. They are built on selective reordering and combinatory play. Peter Gizzi's *Ode: Salute to the New York School* (2012) and Simone Muench's *Wolf Centos* (2014) are recent, book-length explorations of the form's possibilities, and can serve as an entry point to the power of this patchwork form. Pull a sample of books from the library's poetry collection that represents a range of traditions and give participants twenty minutes to a half-hour to sift through what is there, with open notebooks to record potentially usable lines. Everyone should assemble at least one cento (of any length), and those who want to can share them aloud.

INTERVIEWING AS AN
INFORMATION-GATHERING STRATEGY

Although research is often conceptualized as a library-based process, one that involves, if not books and old letters, databases replete with untold amounts of digitized articles, there are occasions, topics, and genres that lead writers to draw on interviews for information. Writers may want to consider how to engage people face-to-face for the facts and perspectives they can offer. If a library hosts writers who are interested in family or local history, for example, the salient details about their subjects will likely include individuals, regardless of what has been preserved in newspaper stories or archival sources. This brief guidance on supporting writers' preparations for informational interviewing emphasizes core activities, and where ideas and information about those endeavors can be found.

Noting the ways that historians draw on interviews, James Beilman called upon a long-standing description of the interview as dependent upon "a systematic collection, arrangement, preservation, and publication" of its subject's thoughts.[5] Beilman emphasizes the interview's afterlife in the form of a record, alongside the importance of critical and contextual thinking that will surround the creation of this record. On a basic level, each time a writer conducts an interview she must decide how to record her notes. This invites an enduring and fundamental question: should an interviewer take notes by hand or rely on a recording technology? This is a question that different people answer differently, reflecting their working habits, the publication culture they respond to, and related considerations.

We offer the following details on the question. In a chapter called "Elicitation" from *Draft No. 4* (2017), John McPhee explains his preference for taking notes by hand during interviews. He describes the way an interviewer's notebook and note-taking habits figure in the dynamic of an informational interview. The exception to his normal processes is the scientific or technical interview, where terminology, both meaning and spelling, may prove challenging to the average author. Writers who wish to make voice or video recordings should express that interest when they make an appointment to meet with someone. It is also worth remembering that many publishers will ask authors to obtain signed permissions from people who are interviewed for a story or a book. Numerous websites offer sample forms, if the publisher does not provide them or if the writer is early in his process.

Beyond the process of documenting an interview, the questions a writer asks also require forethought and preparation. Two broad categories of information support an information-seeking interview: details about an individual's background, and those that help a researcher understand the subject matter of that person's expertise. When seeking information on an individual, any number of websites list an individual's credentials and title. Verifying salient details, though, ensures that any resources consulted contain current information. For content-area knowledge, one direction of research would be a quick search to see whether the subject appears in recent news stories, if it is somehow involved in current controversies, or reporting on recent events. Otherwise, specialized encyclopedias, in particular, can adeptly outline a complex subject for a novice, creating a baseline of information and awareness of related terminology likely to arise during an interview.

When it comes to the questions researchers should ask, the purpose of the interview and the relationship between the interviewer and interviewee will create wide variations. If a writer is pursuing a family-history project, it might make sense to first access oral histories published online, either as audio files or transcriptions, in order to develop a sense of the genre, like those provided on fandom or labor history in the Iowa Digital Library.[6] The Oral History Association identifies online resources to support this sort of endeavor, and the UCLA Library's Center for Oral History Research provides a detailed discussion of how this sort of interview should proceed.[7] If the subject is a more distant one, writers will have to devise a plan relative to the purpose of their projects, considering what they might learn from this individual that they could not glean elsewhere. Broadly, however, we might help writers think about the difference between open-ended and closed questions, or those that invite interviewees to expand on a subject and those which do not, as well as biased or leading questions, which might rankle the hearer or suggest that the interviewer's stance will overwrite the interviewee's opinions.

# Writing Groups

One reality of writing is that few pieces will see publication without editing and feedback. Although professional editors or agents will, inevitably, be part of this process, many writers opt for preliminary feedback through writing groups. Writing groups, with their echoes of the Bloomsbury salons or fireside gatherings in Lord Byron's villa where Mary Shelley's *Frankenstein* was first read, may seem like the sort of environment where lively, engaged conversation about literary work flows naturally. The reality is that without planning, a writing group will serve few people's creative aims. While librarians might invite the initial participants to shape the ground rules for the group, everyone who participates in the group needs to understand and operate according to these conventions.

Writers can be of two minds about sharing their work in these settings. Some feel that they've put their heart and soul into a narrative or a poem, crafting and revising until they can do no more; these writers may greet the idea that their hard work needs anything other than an appreciative audience with suspicion. Others feel a pull toward social situations, after many hours spent writing alone. For people in either category, or those somewhere in between, the feedback garnered from a writers' group may offer rewards, whether it's a first public airing of their ideas or a confirmation that something still remains to be done, despite all the work that's gone into getting to this point. While the culture of any given group can vary, one that provides writers with useful ways to think about their next steps typically relies on some fundamental strategies to organize its workings.

Each critique group needs a leader to facilitate its functioning. Moreover, while it is possible to have less formal operations, typically, a group needs a schedule for its sessions. A librarian serving as moderator must keep track of time during a critique session and be prepared to intervene in the conversation in order to maintain a schedule and to ensure that the group's protocols are observed. The details of a writer's conduct, the group's processes, and resources that offer further guidance augment these broad responsibilities.

It can be helpful to hear the writer read a brief passage from his or her work at the outset of the critique, and then ask questions of the participants for a set amount of time at the conclusion, but the writer should otherwise remain silent during the discussion. This can be difficult but it is crucial. For the writer, the opportunity to hear what it's like for others to make sense of the text and to think about how they came to their respective readings is both uncomfortable and indispensable. Waiting until the conclusion of the discussion to ask a few questions in turn is a small price to pay for this. Also, if the writer embarks on a defense of what's on the page or argues with the commenters, it's likely to derail the group's time constraints.

As to the purpose of questions at the end of a critique: the writer may benefit from asking specific, concrete questions about how people experienced the piece or about speculative changes. Writers may have particular problems they've been trying to fix over multiple drafts, and direct questions about these points can be indispensable. It should be made clear that this is not a venue for offering corrections or cross-examinations. Most sources remind authors that in the end, it's up to them to decide what they do with the concerns or praise expressed during these sessions. Particularly if different participants voice divergent reactions, a writer has to decide how feedback supports her larger intention for the project, or if there is a reason to make major changes to her work. She will have a better chance of doing this if she focuses on simply and accurately writing down what is being said in order to consider it later. Noting only what feels immediately correct or helpful presumes that the writer has begun a critique with foreknowledge of these things, which would make the critique largely pointless. This is easily summarized: be a stenographer, not a defense attorney.

Barring a round-robin structure, which focuses on a single writer's work each session, most groups allocate and limit the time for each critique. This pragmatic step assumes that the group's members will have read the material before the meeting and serves many purposes, including ensuring that the group doesn't concentrate the majority of its time on a single piece of writing and thus pay scant attention to others' projects. In addition to the fundamental principle of equity, there is only so much information that a writer can absorb at one time.

A common model for critique meetings has the writer whose work is under discussion listen and observe, while the moderator has each participant identify one specific strength in the work, with concrete examples. Hearing about where even a single word choice resonated for one other reader in the room can give a writer the reassurance she needs in order to remain open to the fact that other moments in the work didn't come together as well and can still be improved. The bulk of the work, in most critiques, is not on reaching a consensus—though some consensus is likely to emerge about some of the broadest problems or successes of a piece. Instead, the challenge that participants have is to articulate and justify *why* they think what they do with as much specificity, care, and honesty as possible.

Alternately, rather than having each participant react to the whole of the work, the moderator can plan a session with committed participants by directing each person to focus on a different portion of the piece, giving it a close reading. Still another option is to assign specific technical elements to different participants to lead the discussion on (narrative point of view, dialogue, setting, imagery). This strategy ensures that feedback is distributed and attends to a variety of aspects of a draft, rather than clustering around a single aspect of the work in progress. Yet depending on the length of the work, some attempt to talk briefly about the whole may also be worth attempting in order to avoid a disjointed critique. Following the evaluation, the librarian-moderator would invite everyone to give one suggestion for the next draft.

The language that participants use during critiques is important. Most advice begins with the premise that those who offer feedback need to consider the effect of what they say. In general, it is more useful for participants to couch their feedback in terms of the manuscript rather than its author and to avoid the imperative mood and second-person utterances. Those taking part in these discussions should keep in mind how it would feel to hear more abrupt remarks about their own creative work and to describe their criticisms as their own reactions, rather than as intrinsic properties of the work or its author. It is beneficial for participants to be precise, rather than vague, in both their praise and negative comments; focusing on a moment in the plot, a phrase, or some specific element rather than on the general language of the piece or on one's emotional response to a character, offers the writer a clearer direction for potential changes.[8]

Beyond these fundamentals, there are a number of resources that discuss the logistics of group critiques, and they may offer useful details and perspective on process:

- Organizers at the Des Moines Writers Workshop divide their advice into sections that focus on overall meeting structure, delivering effective critiques, and listening to critical comments about one's writing (http://desmoineswritersworkshop.com/critique-group-guidelines/).

- The Writers Loft in Massachusetts augments its concise ideas with a list of further sources to consult if you want to develop a more robust sense of how critique groups work (https://www.thewritersloft.org/critique).

- The SLO NightWriters group in California has a more discursive, empathetic description of how writers and critique sessions work, yet its overview includes many good, pragmatic details to consider in forming and maintaining a writers' group (www.slonightwriters.org/page-1124948).

- *Writer's Digest* is a standard periodical resource for those undertaking professional creative writing, regardless of genre. While a piece was posted on a *WD* blog with a title proclaiming that "There Are No Rules," its author nonetheless derives some operating principles based on her personal experience with writing groups. Her ideas focus on managing the multiple and sometimes conflicting opinions that emerge from critiques (www.writersdigest.com/editor-blogs/there-are-no-rules/guest-post/4-ways-to-make-the-most-of-a-critique-group).

Our ability to aid writers in their creative work serves multiple ends. It encourages individuals' familiarity with library sources and services, inviting users to see the library and its staff as responsive and supportive. It recognizes interrelated roles and processes of consuming and creating, encouraging writers and makers to see the library in new ways. Finally, it helps writers and readers connect, making the library a site that helps develop communities of practice.

Aspiring writers and creators all have their own individual ideas of purpose and success. Some want to craft personal stories to share with those closest to them, while others want to see their works on bestseller lists and library shelves. We know that the publishing industry is competitive and its dynamics are changing, so those who measure the value of their words by literary stardom have a long and difficult road ahead of them, along which the library can offer support and from which it can offer respite. By supporting creative communities, we offer a place where patrons can work or rest, as they head toward destinations they determine for themselves. Regardless of the wider world's reception of their work, by fostering communities of practice, we can assist them in renewing their ideas, connections, and spirit of creation, as they read, research, and write.

Notes

1. Jennifer Egan, "Open Shelves," *New York Times Book Review* (November 26, 2017), 27.

2. Anthony Doerr, *Four Seasons in Rome* (New York: Simon & Schuster, 2008), 30, 21.

3. Quoted in Alanna Okun, "7 Times Knitting Was Mocked in Popular Culture," Buzzfeed (July 29, 2013), https://www.buzzfeed.com/alannaokun/7-times-knitting-was-mocked-in-popular-culture.

4. David Shields's essay can be found in *Remote* (University of Wisconsin Press, 1996).

5. James Beilman, "The University of Iowa Oral History Project," *Books at Iowa* 27, no. 1: 22, http://ir.uiowa.edu/bai/v0127/iss1.

6. Media Fandom Oral History Project, https://digital.lib.uiowa.edu/cdm/search/collection/fohp; and Iowa Labor Oral History Project, http://digital.lib.uiowa.edu/cdm/landingpage/collection/ilhop.

7. "Web Guides to Doing Oral History," Oral History Association (August 2012), www.oralhistory.org/web-guides-to-doing-oral-history/; "Interviewing Guidelines," UCLA Library Center for Oral History Research (n.d.), http://oralhistory.library.ucla.edu/interviewGuidelines.html#info.

8. Lex Williford and Michael Martone, eds., "A Workshop Guide for Creative Writing," in *Touchstone Anthology of Contemporary Creative Nonfiction* (Touchstone, 2007) models questions and elements for participants.

Books and Other Sources on Writing

If you plan to support writers by providing information resources, the following texts and resources can be useful to both aspiring and established writers. While few books or online resources will suit every writer's needs, we have identified a cluster of well-regarded and regularly referenced materials. Most are contemporary, many are classics, and some, like *Writer's Market*, are reissued annually or updated online. These materials treat a wide variety of literary genres, as understood by experienced writers and editors. More detailed bibliographies, which explore life-writing and writing about art, are available online at https://ir.uiowa.edu/slis_pubs/20/ and https://ir.uiowa.edu/slis_pubs/19.

American Library Association, Resource Guide. www.ala.org/advocacy/advleg/publicawareness/campaign@yourlibrary/sponsorship/putwritingbibliography.

Baxter, Charles. *The Art of Subtext: Beyond Plot* (Minneapolis, MN: Graywolf, 2007).

———. *Burning Down the House: Essays on Fiction* (Minneapolis, MN: Graywolf, 2008).

Birkerts, Sven. *The Art of Time in Memoir: Then, Again* (Minneapolis, MN: Graywolf, 2007).

Bram, Christopher. *The Art of History: Unlocking the Past in Fiction & Nonfiction* (Minneapolis, MN: Graywolf, 2016).

Casey, Maud. *The Art of Mystery: The Search for Questions* (Minneapolis, MN: Graywolf, 2018).

Castellani, Christopher. *The Art of Perspective: Who Tells the Story* (Minneapolis, MN: Graywolf, 2016).

Danticat, Edwidge. *The Art of Death: Writing the Final Story* (Minneapolis, MN: Graywolf, 2017).

———. *Create Dangerously: The Immigrant Artist at Work* (New York: Vintage, 2011).

D'Erasmo, Stacey. *The Art of Intimacy: The Space Between* (Minneapolis, MN: Graywolf, 2013).

Doty, Mark. *The Art of Description: World into Word* (Minneapolis, MN: Graywolf, 2010).

Dufresne, John. *The Lie That Tells a Truth: A Guide to Writing Fiction* (New York: W.W. Norton, 2003).

Elliott, Zetta. "The Writer's Page: Decolonizing the Imagination." *Horn Book* (March 2, 2010), https://www.hbook.com/2010/03/authors-illustrators/decolonizing-imagination/.

Fussell, Paul. *Poetic Meter and Poetic Form* (New York: Random House, 1979).

Heaney, Katie. "Just Write 500 Words." The Cut (June 11, 2018). https://www.thecut.com/2018/06/if-you-want-to-write-a-book-write-500-words-a-day.html

Hemley, Robin. *Turning Life into Fiction* (Minneapolis, MN: Graywolf, 2006).

Hoagland, Tony. *Real Sofistikashun: Essays on Poetry and Craft* (Minneapolis, MN: Graywolf, 2006).

Hugo, Richard. *The Triggering Town: Lectures and Essays on Poetry and Writing* (New York: W.W. Norton, 1992).

Koch, Kenneth. *Rose, Where Did You Get That Red? Teaching Great Poetry to Children* (New York: Vintage, 2012).

Lerner, Betsy. *The Forest for the Trees: An Editor's Advice to Writers, Revised* (New York: Riverhead Books, 2010).

Lopate, Phillip, ed. *The Art of the Personal Essay: An Anthology from the Classical Era to the Present* (New York: Anchor, 1995).

McCann, Colum. *Letters to a Young Writer: Some Practical and Philosophical Advice* (New York: Random House, 2017).

Phillips, Carl. *The Art of Daring: Risk, Restlessness, Imagination* (Minneapolis, MN: Graywolf, 2014).

Revell, Donald. *The Art of Attention: A Poet's Eye* (Minneapolis, MN: Graywolf, 2007).

Rilke, Rainer Maria. *Letters to a Young Poet*, trans. Michel Stephens (New York: Modern Library, 1984).

Silber, Joan. *The Art of Time in Fiction: As Long as It Takes* (Minneapolis, MN: Graywolf, 2009).

Stern, Jerome. *Making Shapely Fiction* (New York: W.W. Norton, 2011).

Strand, Mark, and Eavan Boland, eds. *The Making of a Poem: A Norton Anthology of Poetic Forms* (New York: W.W. Norton, 2000).

Verma, Henrietta. "Writer Here: Programming," *Library Journal* (August 15, 2016) https://www.libraryjournal.com/?detailStory=write-here-programming.

Voigt, Ellen Bryant. *The Art of Syntax: Rhythm of Thought, Rhythm of Song* (Minneapolis, MN: Graywolf, 2009).

Writer's Market (Writer's Digest Books).

Young, Dean. *The Art of Recklessness: Poetry as Assertive Force and Contradiction* (Minneapolis, MN: Graywolf, 2010).

APPENDIX

B

Rhyme and Meter

Rhyme and meter used to be poets' bread and butter. After the advent of free verse, they've largely taken a back seat to other generative practices and means of constraint. There are still contemporary American poets who employ rhyme and meter, like Greg Williamson and Marilyn Hacker, but most practicing poets have opted for other forms. You'll likely have many participants in your library who still associate poetry with the likes of Henry Wadsworth Longfellow and Robert Frost, and these participants will still want to work by matching sounds and counting beats. You should remember that working with rhyme and meter written in English may be difficult for participants for whom English is a second language. Moreover, even native speakers of English can sometimes fail to grasp the language's cadences in ways they can replicate in verse.

An excellent, comprehensive guide to meter is Paul Fussell's *Poetic Meter and Poetic Form* (1979), which enumerates four types of meter: syllabic, accentual, accentual-syllabic, and "quantitative." The first three of these will be sufficient for your group's participants.

■ Syllabic meter is meter that counts syllables without regard to accents or beats. This is how most people in the Anglophone world produce haiku: by counting 5–7–5 syllables. But if you're looking for other examples, try Marianne Moore's "The Fish," whose every stanza adheres to a 1–3–9–6–9

179

syllable count. Syllabic meter might be the easiest to work with for beginners.

▨ Accentual meter is meter that counts accents or beats without regard to the number of syllables. This might be trickier for beginners, because the same number of syllables can have different numbers of beats. "Is this the face that launched a thousand ships?" contains ten syllables and five beats:

> is THIS the FACE that LAUNCH'D a THOUsand SHIPS?

The sentence, "How are you doing today, Dorothy?" contains ten syllables and only four beats: HOW are you DO ing to DAY, DOR o thy? That is, accentual meter counts only how many verbal stresses are in a line. For an example, use William Carlos Williams' cheeky "This Is Just to Say," which contains variable syllables per line, but only one beat which is represented in bold :

> I have **ea**ten
> the **plums**
> that were **in**
> the **ice**box
>
> and **which**
> you were **prob**ably
> **sa**ving
> for **break**fast
>
> For**give** me
> they were de**li**cious
> so **sweet**
> and so **cold**

▨ Accentual-syllabic meter is meter that counts both accents and syllables together. This produces more formal Anglophone meters such as iambic pentameter. Within a line of iambic pentameter there are generally five stresses and ten syllables, with every other syllable stressed or unstressed, beginning with an unstressed syllable: "Is **this** the **face** that **launch'd** a **thou**sand **ships**?" Rather than taking the substantial time to educate yourself on all the accentual-syllabic meters (trochaic tetrameter, dactylic trimeter, etc.), it's easier to simply find poems written in accentual-syllabic meters and replicate them. Technically, Robert Frost's "Stopping by Woods on a Snowy Evening" is written in a meter called iambic tetrameter. For your writing group, it should suffice just to puzzle out the pattern of stresses and syllables and try to mimic it:

> Whose **woods** these **are** I **think** I **know.**
> His **house** is **in** the **vill**age **though;**
> He **will** not **see** me **stop**ping **here**
> To **watch** his **woods** fill **up** with **snow.**

The above example, in addition to having a uniform meter, also has a rhyme scheme. The end words *know, though,* and *snow* rhyme, and *here* produces an unrhyming sound that will be used in the second stanza. When figuring a rhyme scheme, practitioners use letters for each new rhyme sound that end words produce. So in this case, the scheme would be AABA. If you were to read on to the next stanza, you would see that it continues BBCB, then CCDC, and so on. Rhyme tends to be a lot more accessible to participants than meter, but typically the participants who enjoy working with one will enjoy working with both.

 ## "The Red Wheelbarrow"

You can investigate the meter used in William Carlos Williams's famous "The Red Wheelbarrow":

> so much depends
>
> upon
>
> a red wheel
>
> barrow

glazed with rain
water

beside the white
chickens.

Are there a uniform number of syllables per line or stanza? Are there a uniform number of stresses or beats? If so, is the meter syllabic, accentual, or accentual-syllabic?

Answer: There are not a uniform number of syllables, but there are a uniform number of stresses. Each couplet contains a stress count of two stresses in the first line and one in the second, or 2–1. Thus, this poem employs accentual meter.

Once your group has identified the meter of the poem, they can replicate it in their own original poems, writing four couplets with a 2–1 accentual meter: so **much** de**pends** / up**on** // a **red wheel** / **bar**row // **glazed** with **rain** / **wa**ter // be**side** the **white** / **chick**ens. ◢◤◤

INHERITED VERSE FORMS

Sometimes used in tandem with rhyme and meter, sometimes using one or the other, and sometimes simply using repeated words, inherited forms like sonnets, villanelles, sestinas, and pantoums continue to captivate modern and contemporary American poets like Elizabeth Bishop, Natalie Diaz, Latasha N Nevada Diggs, and others. Inherited forms are forms whose rules or constraints have been passed down to us, though the rules may still be in dispute. There are, for instance, key differences between a Spenserian sonnet and a Shakespearean sonnet. The way sonnets are composed today generally entails a line-count of fourteen and what's called a volta, or a turn in logic, tone, or narrative, between the eighth and ninth lines.

 # The Supersonnet

If your participants are feeling particularly adventurous, your group could add further constraints on top of the inherited forms. For this example, we'll use "Sonnet with a Different Letter at the End of Every Line" by George Starbuck:

> O for a muse of fire, a sack of dough,
> Or both! O promissory notes of woe!
> One time in Santa Fe N.M.
> Ol' Winfield Townley Scott and I . . . But whoa.
> One can exert oneself, *ff,*
> Or architect a heaven like Rimbaud,
> Or if that seems, how shall I say, *de trop,*
> One can at least write sonnets, a propos
> Of nothing save the do-re-mi-fa-sol
> Of poetry itself. Is not the row
> Of perfect rhymes, the terminal bon mot,
> Obeisance enough to the Great O?
> "Observe," said Chairman Mao to Premier Chou,
> "On voyage à Parnasse pour prendre les eaux.
> On voyage comme poisson, incog."

Starbuck couldn't help himself and added a fifteenth line to his improvised sonnet, but he included two other constraints: (1) the beginning of every line starts with the letter "O"; and (2) every line ends with a long -o- sound while ending with a different letter of the alphabet.

With your group, read and discuss Starbuck's sonnet. Then decide on two constraints of your own to add to a sonnet and produce your own. These further constraints might include having every line contain a film title, making it an abecedarian by beginning each line with a different letter in alphabetical order, or using the word "cucumber" in every stanza.

The rules for each verse form are easy to find on the Web, especially via institutions like the Academy of American Poets:

The Sonnet
(https://www.poets.org/poetsorg/text/sonnet-poetic-form)

The Villanelle
(https://www.poets.org/poetsorg/text/villanelle-poetic-form)
The Sestina
(https://www.poets.org/poetsorg/text/sestina-poetic-form)
The Pantoum
(https://www.poets.org/poetsorg/text/pantoum-poetic-form)
The Ghazal
(https://www.poets.org/poetsorg/text/ghazal-poetic-form)

If you're looking for a one-stop shopping experience for verse forms to have on the shelves, *The Making of a Poem: A Norton Anthology of Poetic Forms* (2000), edited by Mark Strand and Eavan Boland, contain rules, brief histories, and great examples of each inherited form.

A good verse form to begin with might be the sonnet, since it's shorter than most of the other forms, has a more recognizable history insofar as some or many of your participants may have read a Shakespearean sonnet in high school, and is relatively easier to pull off if your group uses only the two rules mentioned above: fourteen lines plus a volta. John Ashbery's "Farm Implements and Rutabagas in a Landscape," which can be found on the Web (https://www.poets.org/poetsorg/poem/farm-implements-and-rutabagas-landscape), usually delights participants as an example of a sestina, since Ashbery uses characters and situations from *Popeye* as his repetends (repeated words):

> The first of the undecoded messages read: "Popeye sits
> in thunder,
> Unthought of. From that shoebox of an apartment,
> From livid curtain's hue, a tangram emerges: a country."
> Meanwhile the Sea Hag was relaxing on a green couch: "How
> pleasant
> To spend one's vacation *en la casa de Popeye*," she
> scratched
> Her cleft chin's solitary hair. She remembered spinach
>
> And was going to ask Wimpy if he had bought any spinach.
> "M'love," he intercepted, "the plains are decked out
> in thunder

Today, and it shall be as you wish." He scratched
The part of his head under his hat. The apartment
Seemed to grow smaller. "But what if no pleasant
Inspiration plunge us now to the stars? *For this is my*
country."

As an example of a villanelle, Elizabeth Bishop's "One Art" is frequently taught and is a stunning, if bleak, realization of the form. Writers who are not too intimidated by her example may find that it also lends itself to elegies.

Invented Forms

In this exercise, your group will invent its own verse form(s).

First, read and examine "Paradelle for Susan" by Billy Collins:

> I remember the quick, nervous bird of your love.
> I remember the quick, nervous bird of your love.
> Always perched on the thinnest, highest branch.
> Always perched on the thinnest, highest branch.
> Thinnest love, remember the quick branch.
> Always nervous, I perched on your highest bird the.
> —
> It is time for me to cross the mountain.
> It is time for me to cross the mountain.
> And find another shore to darken with my pain.
> And find another shore to darken with my pain.
> Another pain for me to darken the mountain.
> And find the time, cross my shore, to with it is to.
> —
> The weather warm, the handwriting familiar.
> The weather warm, the handwriting familiar.
> Your letter flies from my hand into the waters below.
> Your letter flies from my hand into the waters below.

The familiar waters below my warm hand.

Into handwriting your weather flies you letter the from the.

—

I always cross the highest letter, the thinnest bird.

Below the waters of my warm familiar pain,

Another hand to remember your handwriting.

The weather perched for me on the shore.

Quick, your nervous branch flew from love.

Darken the mountain, time and find was my into it was with to to.

In the poem's initial publication, it came with a note by the author:

> The paradelle is one of the more demanding French fixed forms, first appearing in the langue d'oc love poetry of the eleventh century. It is a poem of four six-line stanzas in which the first and second lines, as well as the third and fourth lines of the first three stanzas, must be identical. The fifth and sixth lines, which traditionally resolve these stanzas, must use all the words from the preceding lines and only those words. Similarly, the final stanza must use every word from all the preceding stanzas and only those words.

You may have your participants attempt paradelles of their own, but heed a word of caution: Collins invented the form as a hoax to poke fun at the strictures of the villanelle. So writing one can be very tricky and time-consuming. Instead, it might be better to have your participants invent a form of their own. Then they may either try to write a poem in the form they have invented, or they can trade forms with one another and attempt their colleagues' forms. In sharing the results, you can decide as a group which forms might have a future in the poetic tradition.

SOME BOOK-LENGTH GUIDES FOCUSED ON FORM

- *The Making of a Poem,* ed. Eavan Boland and Mark Strand (2001)
- *Book of Rhymes: The Poetics of Hip Hop,* by Adam Bradley (2017)
- *The Poem's Heartbeat,* by Alfred Corn (2008)
- *A Little Book on Form,* by Robert Hass (2018)
- *Rhyme's Reason,* by John Hollander (2014)
- *The Art of the Poetic Line,* by James Longenbach (2007)
- *Rules for the Dance,* by Mary Oliver (1998)
- *The Teacher's and Writer's Handbook of Poetic Forms,* by Ron Padgett (2000)

ABOUT THE AUTHORS

RILEY HANICK is the author of *Three Kinds of Motion: Kerouac, Pollock, and the Making of American Highways* (2015). His writings have appeared in *Sonora Review*, *Seneca Review*, *No Depression*, *eyeshot*, and *Labor World*. He has received support from the Jentel and McKnight foundations and served as a writer-in-residence for the University of Iowa Museum of Art. His essay "The Pradelles" was among the notable essays in the 2010 Best American series. From 2013 to 2016 he was the nonfiction editor at *New Madrid* and the visiting Watkins Chair in creative writing at Murray State University. He has tutored and helped to facilitate creative writing programs in prisons, public schools, libraries, and domestic violence shelters.

MICAH BATEMAN is a Ph.D. candidate in English at the University of Texas at Austin, where he is an Andrew W. Mellon Engaged Scholar Initiative Fellow and previously served as the assistant director of the New Writers Project MFA program. He is a graduate of the Iowa Writers' Workshop as well as the recipient of the Poetry Society of America's Lyric Poetry Award, and his chapbook of poems, *Polis*, is published by the Catenary Press. Bateman has worked for the Coralville Public Library and the University of Iowa Libraries.

JENNIFER BUREK PIERCE is associate professor in the School of Library and Information Science at the University of Iowa. She developed *American Libraries'* "Youth Matters" column in 2007 and has also written for *Seventeen*, the *Chronicle of Higher Education*, and the *Paris Review Daily*. Her most recent book is *Sex, Brains, and Video Games: Information and Inspiration for Youth Services Librarians* (2017). Fellowships from the American Antiquarian Society and the Winterthur Museum, Library, and Gardens have supported her research on library collections for young people.

INDEX